Dare to Do Only the Father's Will

Living from within His Presence

Suzanne Pillans

GW00546726

New Wine Press

New Wine Ministries
PO Box 17
Chichester
West Sussex
United Kingdom
PO19 2AW

ISBN 978-1-905991-35-8

Typeset by CRB Associates, Reepham, Norfolk
Printed in Malta

Contents

Foreword

I first met Suzanne and her family in February 2001 when they came to one of my meetings in England. She and her husband received healing, and she shared with me her urgent desire to come to our 'Fire over Jerusalem' Convention in May later that same year.

Suzanne is a wife and mother, a hard-working owner of a successful horse- riding school, a quiet but determined person with a great hunger and thirst for God. At the time when I first met her, her key scripture for two years had been John 7:38: *'He who believes in Me, as the Scripture has said, out of his heart will flow rivers of living water'* (NKJV). For two years she had cried out, 'But there's no water flowing through my life!' She read every book on revival, every book on prayer. She came to our 'Fire over Jerusalem' Convention in Israel in May 2001 – and the fire fell – on her!

This book is the evidence of the power and anointing which is flowing through her ministry, firstly in the 'Fire over Kenya' Conference, then wherever she has gone, in Africa and now in India, but also in her own home surroundings, in obedience to the call of God. Suzanne has a very practical experience with the Lord which relates to everyday experience. She shows in this book that God uses the ordinary people to demonstrate His power and glory. When God called an eighty-year-old man called Moses to become the one who would lead the Jewish people out of captivity in Egypt, Moses was just a shepherd with a family to support. The Bible says that not many high or mighty are called, but *'God has chosen the weak to confound the mighty'*.

The ministry and the healings continue, as Suzanne continues to believe God. I have no divine call to India (mine is to Russia and Europe) – but Suzanne does and in a recent Crusade in India, she saw attendances up to 160,000 and almost 100,000 confirmed converts.

The challenge is this; Jesus said: *'He who believes in Me . . . out of his heart will flow rivers of living water.'* Talk is not enough – we need action. Today we have many preachers but too few *evangelists*, who will demonstrate the power of Jesus in the world today! The Holy Spirit is using Suzanne as a true evangelist!

David Hathaway
Evangelist
President of Eurovision

Preface

In the spirit realm I am standing in awe before my Heavenly Father. Holding up to the Father the twelve sayings of Jesus on prayer from the book of John, I say, 'Father God, I have one request. Is it possible to know You more? Is it possible to come to know You even as Jesus knew You through these sayings of His in Scripture?'

'Have I not already revealed My heart to you?'

'Yes, my Father, and this has become the blueprint of my life, the core of my being, the aim of every breath within me, to proclaim Jesus to everyone I can, to somehow relieve the pain of Your intense love mixed with sorrow for mankind, by bringing them to know You in every way I can, following the example of Jesus as the only way.'

'Yes, the example of My Son is truly the only way and your quest to know Me, as My Son Jesus knows me, is right. As you approach Me in the same manner as My Son Jesus, you will touch Me, you will touch Heaven, and, as you do, the reflection of everything you need, to do My work, will radiate through your very being. On your own you can do nothing, but when you touch Me in prayer, as Jesus did, then your inner man becomes full of My resources and you will begin to move into the realm that Jesus My Son lived in. Your request, My child, has been granted.'

A Word from the Author

'Father God, I lift up to You this book which I am writing, the subject of which I have never heard preached on, written about or taught.'

So who am I to write it? A person saved by grace, through what Jesus did on the cross for us, turning me into one of His children to be born to everlasting life. Therefore my eternal home is Heaven, not earth, and I believe the Scriptures are written for our benefit. These sayings of Jesus about *doing only the Father's will* are repeated twelve times in different ways in John's Gospel, to affect every area of our lives. Twelve times in one book speaks of its paramount importance in every way.

To worship God with all our heart is the first commandment and the most important. Worshipping God is more than just saying prayers and then walking off to live our own lives. To truly worship God is to do so with every single area of our being in honest communication with our heart and mind, voice, understanding and spirit, submitted in obedience and in every activity that follows. It is a complete giving of our entire life.

When one actually begins to worship God in this way, something glorious opens up and our whole life becomes transformed into the success of His call on us, enabling us to rise up into a new level and realm of walking that we never thought possible.

As one dies to one's own plans and agenda, and submits totally to God and His plans for our life, being prepared to walk in His way in total obedience, it is *then* that we enter into the greatest challenge and fulfilment of a successful and triumphant walk in Him.

This book will study twelve of Jesus' sayings about *'only doing the Father's will'* and how this affected His miracles, healings and teachings. I go on to share how I have tried to put these verses about *'only doing the Father's will'* into my own life and ministry, and to share with you the outstanding results I have seen. As I practise these sayings on *'only doing the Father's will'* more and more, I am seeing these sayings transform my entire life and ministry and it is my prayer that they will transform your life too.

Seeking God with all your heart, and only doing the Father's will, seems to open the very promises and blessings of Scripture on your life.

Who We Are in Christ

*'John answered and said, A man can receive nothing,
except it be given him from heaven.'*
(John 3:27)

From Heaven? Who are *we* that we should receive from Heaven, it may be asked? Well, that all depends on who we think we are and how we access the heavenly realm in order to receive.

Why did Jesus need to ask the Father about everything He did? Wasn't He the very son of God? Oh yes, He was. But He was also human. He was born into the earthly realm, the physical realm. Only by coming to the Father could He enter the eternal, heavenly realm again, the more powerful realm in which His Father lived.

What I am trying to say is this. When I was a teenager in South Africa, I used to walk in the mountains. I looked around at the beauty around me and sensed that, somehow, behind all that I saw there was something greater and I wanted, beyond all things, to find out what it was.

It wasn't until I was twenty-three years old, after admiring a perfect water lily, that my search was to come to an end. Three weeks later, I went into the Drakensberg Mountains again, this time with my camera, to find the water lily withered and dead. A couple of months later I rode up again and collected a bucket of water for my horse from the same spot, only to see *three* water lilies as perfect as the first one, and I sat down in the heather to admire them. Suddenly a voice, silent, yet unmistakably clear, said, 'As that water lily had to die of itself for its seed to break open and new life to emerge, so I died on the cross that many may have new life in Me.'

Only Jesus died on the cross, so I prayed, 'If that is You, Jesus, may I have this new life as well?' Immediately I was filled with His glorious presence and my life was changed forever. I knew firsthand Who was behind those beautiful mountains, the prancing deer, the glistening waterfalls and the whole of creation and mankind. I had suddenly met with the eternal realm and the God of heaven, the greater force and power. I read the Bible from cover to cover and discovered much that speaks of the two different realms. The God of Heaven with great power and authority Who created the earth in six days by the power of His word. Then Jesus, who walked in great victory, power and authority over every sickness, demonic power, the forces of nature and even death itself. This is the heavenly, eternal realm.

The other realm is the natural, temporal realm that we are born into on earth. Here the people try and decide on things, without the power of God, based only upon their five senses to interpret the material world. Through this limiting view, they cannot get behind what causes sickness or mental problems and spend much money and time studying to overcome them, often only to be beaten by a microscopic germ which is suddenly able to build up resistance to the medicine. This sends the scientists and doctors back to the laboratory to develop a yet stronger medicine!

Jesus, though, had the true answer to all of this. He went to the Father Who endued Him with His glorious presence, power and authority which enabled Jesus to get up off his knees filled with the eternal, heavenly realm of signs and wonders which then followed Him on earth. What is more, He has given you and me the ability to do the same, simply by coming into the Father's presence in prayer to ask the Father just as He did, about everything we need to do.

What are we waiting for? Let's do what Jesus teaches us through these twelve sayings about 'only doing the Father's will'. As for me, I am not going to let anything stop me.

Who we are will determine how we live and who we believe we are will set our course in life. If we believe that we are born of the flesh only, we will live in the limits of the flesh and go after the things of the world. If we just believe what the devil says about us, then we will live in condemnation and guilt (read Revelation 12:10), but if we turn from sin to Jesus and pursue *His* righteousness, then we will see in the Bible who we are *in Christ*, chosen and set apart, sons and daughters of the Living God.

The world, the devil and God say different things about who we are. Jesus clearly believed in a literal Genesis but the world and the present education system teach evolution, instead of creation, which makes people doubt what Genesis says, namely that God created Adam and Eve. If people doubt Adam and Eve, they begin to doubt that Adam and Eve ate from the forbidden tree, thus giving this lovely world over to the devil in exchange for the Knowledge of Good and Evil. As if this is not enough, we are taught to believe that we evolved from monkeys! Yet the Bible says in Genesis 1:26,

> 'And God said, Let us make man in our image, after our likeness: and let them have dominion over the fish of the sea, and over the fowl of the air, and over the cattle, and over all the earth, and over every creeping thing that creepeth upon the earth.'

Now, if we evolved from monkeys, are we going to call our Living God, in whose image we are made and who created

Heaven and Earth, a monkey too? Or are we going to believe what the Scriptures say? After all, where in history has a monkey challenged our authority over the earth, or begun to wear clothes, build a home or create things with his hands? Humans, and humans alone, have the ability to create things with their hands and take authority over the animals of this earth, just as Genesis says. Evolution would also take countless miracles, instead of the one miraculous creation week of Genesis, a literal week as God Himself assures us in the Ten Commandments of Exodus 20:11:

> *'For in six days the LORD made heaven and earth, the sea, and all that in them is, and rested the seventh day: wherefore the LORD blessed the sabbath day, and hallowed it.'*

It should be noted that Jesus took the Ten Commandments literally, for example in Luke 18:18–20:

> *'And a certain ruler asked him, saying, Good Master, what shall I do to inherit eternal life? And Jesus said unto him, Why callest thou me good? none is good, save one, that is, God. Thou knowest the commandments, Do not commit adultery, Do not kill, Do not steal, Do not bear false witness, Honour thy father and thy mother.'*

Besides, if we believe in evolution, then there can be no sin, and we actually end up confusing good with evil or vice versa. By then, we have indeed lost our identity. If we look at our world right now, what do we see? We see people with one big identity crisis! They don't know who they are or who they are descended from, God or a monkey! How then do they behave? Like a human? Or simply an animal, just seeking the pleasures of the moment or losing hope completely? No wonder our young people have taken to drink or drugs. They have no purpose and no future but believe that they are merely born to exist and then to die one day.

The world would have us believe that we are born of the flesh only and anything supernatural that cannot be seen is deemed not to exist, because scientists are unable to prove it. Yet we cannot see air, the wind, radio-waves etc. although we know that they are very real. Can a scientist prove love or hate or the effects of emotional hurt? A scientist can only take what has been always here on the earth and then make something of it for our benefit. How limited is that?

However, the Good News is that we are human beings created in the image of God, with a brain, a choice, and the ability to live as sons and daughters of the Living God, for the Bible says that we are more than just flesh.

So we need to know whether we are spirit beings who live in a body with a soul or, as the world says, just born of the flesh only. The *Oxford Dictionary* defines the spirit as the element in man regarded as separable from the body. This is a very good description. James 2:26 says,

> *'For as the body without the spirit is dead, so faith without works is dead also.'*

Ecclesiastes 12:7 says,

> *'Then shall the dust return to the earth as it was: and the spirit shall return unto God who gave it.'*

This says that we are actually spirits, sent by God to dwell in physical bodies and both the *Oxford Dictionary* and the Bible agree. Hebrews 4:12 says,

> *'For the word of God is quick, and powerful, and sharper than any two-edged sword, piercing even to the dividing asunder of soul and spirit, and of the joints and marrow, and is a discerner of the thoughts and intents of the heart.'*

We have to decide therefore whom to serve, and that determines who we are and to whom we belong. If we choose God, we will belong to Him, and our eternal home will be with Him in Heaven, but, if we choose evil, we will belong to the devil and his home is Hell. In Matthew 6:33 Jesus promises,

> *'But seek ye first the kingdom of God, and his righteousness; and all these things* [that the pagans run after] *shall be added unto you.'*

When Jesus came to earth, man did not simply crucify Jesus. It was the other way round. Jesus *allowed* Himself to be crucified by man so that He could save us, and also show the world Who He really was, the King of kings and Lord of lords. He came to die on the cross as the only perfect sacrifice that could wipe away the sins of man, and give those of us who accept Him as Lord and Saviour a second chance to come into eternal life *in Him*.

1 Timothy 6:15 says,

> *'Which in his times he shall shew, who is the blessed and only Potentate, the King of kings, and Lord of lords.'*

Jesus Himself is His Father's perfect plan for mankind in John 3:16–17,

> *'For God so loved the world, that he gave his only begotten Son, that whosoever believeth in him should not perish, but have everlasting life. For God sent not his Son into the world to condemn the world; but that the world through him might be saved.'*

Jesus rose from the dead in complete victory over every sin, every sickness, and every demonic force. He has ascended into Heaven, where He sits at the right hand of the Father and, according to Ephesians 1:21, He is

'Far above all principality, and power, and might, and dominion, and every name that is named, not only in this world, but also in that which is to come.'

Paul explains this further in Philippians 2:8–11,

'And being found in fashion as a man, he humbled himself, and became obedient unto death, even the death of the cross. Wherefore God also hath highly exalted him, and given him a name which is above every name: That at the name of Jesus every knee should bow, of things in heaven, and things in earth, and things under the earth; And that every tongue should confess that Jesus Christ is Lord, to the glory of God the Father.'

Every sickness has a name, every demon has a name and all must obey the Name of Jesus. If we belong to Jesus, Ephesians 2:1–6 says,

'And you hath he quickened, who were dead in trespasses and sins; Wherein in time past ye walked according to the course of this world, according to the prince of the power of the air, the spirit that now worketh in the children of disobedience: Among whom also we all had our conversation in times past in the lusts of our flesh, fulfilling the desires of the flesh and of the mind; and were by nature the children of wrath, even as others. **But God,** *who is rich in mercy, for his great love wherewith he loved us, even when we were dead in sins, hath quickened us together with Christ, (by grace ye are saved;) And hath raised us up together, and made us sit together in heavenly places in Christ Jesus.'* (emphasis added)

In Luke 10:19 Jesus promised His seventy followers,

'Behold, I give unto you power to tread on serpents and scorpions, and over all the power of the enemy: and nothing shall by any means hurt you.'

Now, coming into that place of receiving is described in Hebrews 2:6–9 which says,

> *'But one in a certain place testified, saying, What is man, that thou art mindful of him? Or the son of man, that thou visitest him? Thou madest him a little lower than the angels; thou crownedst him with glory and honour, and didst set him over the works of thy hands: Thou hast put all things in subjection under his feet. For in that he put all in subjection under him, he left nothing that is not put under him. But now we see not yet all things put under him. But we see Jesus, who was made a little lower than the angels for the suffering of death, crowned with glory and honour; that he by the grace of God should taste death for every man.'*

We have the ability to access Heaven in prayer and to receive and bring the blessings of Heaven down to earth and we are also given the authority of the name of Jesus to bring change to this earth.

As we go to God in prayer, God Himself, the source of all things, will show us what to do, what to say, where to go. He wants to bless others through our lives. Before God, we need to be people of prayer, knowing how to access Heaven. Before our fellow man, we need to have a servant heart, seeking to help and serve and bring man to the knowledge of God. Before the powers of Hell, Jesus has given us authority to rule, to cast out sickness and pain, demons and evil spirits and then to command bodies to be healed physically and to be set free spiritually. God has given us everything we need: Jesus His Son, the authority, the Holy Spirit, the power, the Bible as revealer of truth and the ability to access God's presence in prayer.

We can live with Christ in prayer spiritually even as we live in our physical bodies. Our spirits can soar up in prayer as on spiritual wings right into God's presence. It is here that we meet with God, hear His instruction and are filled with His powerful Holy Spirit, Who will enable us fully to do His work on earth.

To illustrate this further, I would like to share this story. A farmer rescued an injured young eagle and, once the bird was well enough to walk on its injured leg, the farmer put the bird with his chickens to grow up with them. Every day the eagle would go out with the chickens to scratch and peck all day for food on the ground and every night he would return to the chicken hutch with the chickens. This was all the eagle knew, for he had lost his eagle parents. All he knew was what he had learnt from the chickens, how to scratch and peck for food. Then one day, out in the farmyard, a storm began to brew up. The wind blew and the black clouds threatened and all the chickens ran for cover, but the eagle just stood there staring up at the black clouds. He didn't want to run for cover. Something inside him told him he was born for something higher. The eagle began to run around the farmyard with his wings spread for flight and suddenly he rose up from the ground and into the storm. And then above the storm. Suddenly the eagle had found his identity. He was no chicken but an eagle, born to face the storms of life and rise up above them in victory.

Have you found your identity? Or are you still wandering around with the chickens of the world, concentrating only on the knowledge given by the world? Or, put another way, have you found your identity in Christ? Are you able to soar up above the storms of life, in a new dimension of victory in Him?

Once we know who we are in Christ, we will understand like Jesus that *'a man can receive nothing except it be given him from heaven'*. Let us now see how Jesus applied this to His own life. Let us look at Jesus' very first miracle in John 2:3–10.

> *'And when they wanted wine, the mother of Jesus saith unto him, They have no wine. Jesus saith unto her, Woman, what have I to do with thee? mine hour is not yet come. His mother saith unto the*

servants, Whatsoever he saith unto you, do it. And there were set there six waterpots of stone, after the manner of the purifying of the Jews, containing two or three firkins apiece. Jesus saith unto them, Fill the waterpots with water. And they filled them up to the brim. And he saith unto them, Draw out now, and bear unto the governor of the feast. And they bare it. When the ruler of the feast had tasted the water that was made wine, and knew not whence it was: (but the servants which drew the water knew;) the governor of the feast called the bridegroom, And saith unto him, Every man at the beginning doth set forth good wine; and when men have well drunk, then that which is worse: but thou hast kept the good wine until now.'

There is something very interesting here. See how Jesus answers His mother. *'Woman, what have I to do with thee? mine hour is not yet come.'* Jesus had not at that point heard from God. And without God, Jesus could do nothing, for His time had not yet come. But Mary took no notice, she had faith and could not wait much longer for her prophecy that Jesus could do miracles, for she said to the servants, *'Whatsoever he saith unto you, do it.'* What happened here? Was God so impressed with Mary's faith that He changed His mind? After all, God had changed His mind with the prophets in the Old Testament, such as Moses who pleaded with God not to wipe out the people as described in Exodus 32:11–13 or like Abraham in Genesis 18:23–25 when he pleaded with God to spare the righteous in Sodom. I believe God changed His mind because in the next verse Jesus told the servants, *'Fill the waterpots with water.'* Had Jesus now heard the Father say this? I believe so. Jesus next told the servants, *'Draw out now, and bear unto the governor of the feast.'* Suddenly the water was turned into wine. Right from the first miracle, Jesus only did what the Father told Him.

The other question is 'Why should God change His mind?' And He showed me that a parent will sometimes change his or her mind for a child if they see a good motive or if they

want the child to learn something. So it is with God. Out of
His love for us, and His interaction with us, He will allow us
to put forward our ideas and will actually meet with us and
change His mind for our benefit.

In the following verses, we see more fully how Jesus heard
God. John 4:49–54 says,

> *'The nobleman saith unto him, Sir, come down ere my child die.*
> *Jesus saith unto him, Go thy way; thy son liveth. And the man*
> *believed the word that Jesus had spoken unto him, and he went his*
> *way. And as he was now going down, his servants met him, and told*
> *him, saying, Thy son liveth. Then enquired he of them the hour*
> *when he began to amend. And they said unto him, Yesterday at the*
> *seventh hour the fever left him. So the father knew that it was at*
> *the same hour, in the which Jesus said unto him, Thy son liveth: and*
> *himself believed, and his whole house. This is again the second*
> *miracle that Jesus did, when he was come out of Judaea into Galilee.'*

People may ask 'How do you know that Jesus heard God?'
This is answered by John the Baptist in John 3:31–36,

> *'He that cometh from above is above all: he that is of the earth*
> *is earthly, and speaketh of the earth: he that cometh from heaven is*
> *above all. And what he hath seen and heard, that he testifieth; and*
> *no man receiveth his testimony. He that hath received his testimony*
> *hath set to his seal that God is true. For he whom God hath sent*
> *speaketh the words of God: for God giveth not the Spirit by measure*
> *unto him. The Father loveth the Son, and hath given all things into*
> *his hand. He that believeth on the Son hath everlasting life: and he*
> *that believeth not the Son shall not see life; but the wrath of God*
> *abideth on him.'*

Here we can see plainly that Jesus heard from the Father and
spoke the words of the Father, His Father, Who created
heaven and earth by His word.

In John 5, Jesus goes even further. At the pool called Bethesda, there was a certain man who had been disabled for thirty-eight years.

> 'When Jesus saw him lie, and knew that he had been now a long time in that case, he saith unto him, Wilt thou be made whole?'
>
> (John 5:6)

Jesus already knew that God would heal him but now Jesus asked if the man wanted to be healed. In verses 7–9 the disabled man answered Him,

> 'Sir, I have no man, when the water is troubled, to put me into the pool: but while I am coming, another steppeth down before me. Jesus saith unto him, Rise, take up thy bed, and walk. And immediately the man was made whole, and took up his bed, and walked.'

As the Father interacts with mankind, so Jesus does as well, by asking questions before healing people. If we go back to John 4:23, Jesus speaks about us as worshippers:

> 'But the hour cometh, and now is, when the true worshippers shall worship the Father in spirit and in truth: for the Father seeketh such to worship him. God is a Spirit: and they that worship him must worship him in spirit and in truth.'

Only if we know how to worship God, in spirit and in truth, will we be able to hear Him and serve Him, as John 4:35 says,

> 'Say not ye, There are yet four months, and then cometh harvest? behold, I say unto you, Lift up your eyes, and look on the fields; for they are white already to harvest.'

If we now go back to Jesus healing the man by the pool of Bethesda, we read in John 5:16–17:

'And therefore did the Jews persecute Jesus, and sought to slay him, because he had done these things on the sabbath day. But Jesus answered them, My Father worketh hitherto, and I work.'

Even today, the Father is still working.

While in Uganda in 2005 the Lord said to me, 'I want you to reach every village in Uganda.' 'That is impossible', I replied. 'It would take two lifetimes to do that!' 'I will show you how', the Lord replied. Within a week He raised up fifty evangelists to do the job, thirty in Kenya and twenty in Uganda. There was one problem, the reason it had never been done up to now. The distances involved are simply too far to walk during the period between Friday evening and Monday morning. If only they had a bicycle! Well, I could do something about that and sent them enough money from England for twenty-two bicycles and within six months they had planted fifty-four churches. In 2006 we sent a hundred bicycles and they planted 233 churches. In 2007, 301 bicycles were sent and 458 churches were planted, and in 2008, 800 bicycles were sent and 10,000 churches were planted! I had never fundraised before but, out of this, the Lord raised up an entire ministry, complete with a training programme and bicycles to plant churches in every region of eighteen countries.

A man can receive nothing except it be given him from heaven, yet, as 'eagle Christians', we can soar up in prayer and receive from Christ all that He wants to give us. In the next chapter we shall discover how to access heaven and how to receive from God.

Some questions to think about:

- Who does the world say we are?
- Who does the devil say we are?
- Who does God say we are?
- Who do you say you are?

How to See with Your Understanding

> *'Then answered Jesus and said unto them, Verily, verily,*
> *I say unto you, The Son can do nothing of himself, but what*
> *he seeth the Father do: for what things soever he doeth,*
> *these also doeth the Son likewise.'*
> (John 5:19)

Paul says, in 1 Corinthians 2:12,

> *'Now we have received, not the spirit of the world, but the spirit*
> *which is of God; that we might know the things that are freely given*
> *to us of God.'*

If we have accepted Jesus as Lord and Saviour and been baptised in the Holy Spirit, then we may come to God and know the things that are freely given to us by God. How do we access Heaven? By learning to enter the presence of God is to access Heaven and I have written the book *Dare to Enter His Presence* which deals with this in detail. Briefly, there are three steps, as the Tabernacle of the Old Testament shows.

The Outer Court was for the sacrifice of animals, mostly sheep and goats for the forgiveness of sin, but the moment Jesus died on the cross, He became the perfect sacrifice.

'But Christ being come an high priest of good things to come, by a greater and more perfect tabernacle, not made with hands, that is to say, not of this building; neither by the blood of goats and calves, but by his own blood he entered in once into the holy place, having obtained eternal redemption for us. For if the blood of bulls and of goats, and the ashes of an heifer sprinkling the unclean, sanctifieth to the purifying of the flesh: how much more shall the blood of Christ, who through the eternal Spirit offered himself without spot to God, purge your conscience from dead works to serve the living God?' (Hebrews 9:11–14)

So the first step is through the cross, through asking the Lord to forgive anything that we have done wrong.

We can then go into the Inner Court. Psalm 100:4 says,

'Enter into his gates with thanksgiving, and into his courts with praise: be thankful unto him, and bless his name.'

This is where we thank the Lord for what He has done for us and praise Him for Who He is. This is also where many pray for their families, friends, country etc. But there is one problem which causes many people to stop. These people do not realise that there is another dimension, another room, the Holy of Holies. In the Old Testament the priest would enter the Holy of Holies once a year, but the moment Jesus died on the cross the curtain into the Holy of Holies was torn from top to bottom, allowing every one of us into the glorious presence of God. We know it when we enter in. God's presence and His love enfolds us, His peace that passes understanding fills our hearts, and His inner joy, that can be compared with nothing on earth, overflows with fulfilment in Him. This is the beginning of the most glorious relationship with our Father in Heaven, so that all eternity will not see any end to our growing in it. This is where *true* worship starts. This is the place that becomes central to our whole being, here on earth and for all eternity. For me, this has become my home. When my daughter, Rebecca, comes home, the first thing she does is rush upstairs to put her bags in her room, then downstairs to say hello to everyone and after a couple of hugs, she puts the TV on, curls up on the settee and falls asleep. She has come home. She is tired after a busy week at school. Now at home she can rest. In the same way, I feel like Rebecca often when I come into the Lord's presence and the first thing I like to do is simply rest in His presence and enjoy Him. Here is rest indeed.

Let us look at Matthew 11:27,

> *'All things are delivered unto me of my Father: and no man knoweth the Son, but the Father; neither knoweth any man the Father, save the Son, and he to whomsoever the Son will reveal Him.'*

We come to know the Father through Jesus, who reveals the Father to those of us who have received Jesus as our Lord and Saviour. Jesus Himself invites us in the next verses,

> *'Come unto me, all ye that labour and are heavy laden, and I will give you rest. Take my yoke upon you, and learn of me; for I am meek and lowly in heart: and ye shall find rest unto your souls. For my yoke is easy, and my burden is light.'*   (Matthew 11:28–30)

Yes, the first thing I do in the Lord's presence is rest. And I find such rest in Him. He calms me, He takes my tiredness and restores me and I enjoy His glorious presence. I then begin to worship and adore Him. And this draws me in further. It is then that the Father begins to reveal things to me and opens the eyes of my understanding to see things in Scripture and in Him that I have never seen before. This is described by Paul in Ephesians 1:17–21,

> *'That the God of our Lord Jesus Christ, the Father of glory, may give unto you the spirit of wisdom and revelation in the knowledge of*

*him: the eyes of your understanding being enlightened; that ye may
know what is the hope of his calling, and what the riches of the glory
of his inheritance in the saints, and what is the exceeding greatness
of his power to us-ward who believe, according to the working of his
mighty power, which he wrought in Christ, when he raised him from
the dead, and set him at his own right hand in the heavenly places,
far above all principality, and power, and might, and dominion, and
every name that is named, not only in this world, but also in that
which is to come: and hath put all things under his feet, and gave
him to be the head over all things to the church, which is his body,
the fulness of him that filleth all in all.'*

This Scripture says so much but, right now, let us discuss the
'eyes of our understanding being enlightened'. I asked the Lord
to explain this to me and this is what He showed me. Our
natural eyes give us understanding as to what is around us. The
blind cannot see or understand what is around them so they will
have to feel their way and feel the different shapes for their mind
to understand what they are touching. Eyes will clearly reveal to
us what is around us, but even so our eyes are limited. We
cannot see through walls, or into a person's heart or into the
future. But when God opens the eyes of our understanding, we
will see far more clearly than the eyes in our heads, for we will
see with the understanding of Heaven, because God Himself
will open the Scriptures to us and show us depths we have never
perceived. He will show us how He sees the problems in the
world and show us our part in bringing His Good News that will
relieve the people's problems. He will show us many things and
allow us to see what He is doing. Once, when in prayer, I had a
split-second vision of Jesus pointing me to the Father. I turned
towards where Jesus pointed and found myself in a white mist. I
could see nothing and I could hear nothing but what I felt
changed my life forever. I felt just one tiny drop of God's
immense love, a love mixed with terrible sorrow, for the
peoples of this earth and I burst into tears.

'I am sorry, I am sorry,' I repeated over and over – what else could I do, for the pain of God's intense love mixed with sorrow was too much for me to bear? Then He showed me that there were millions of people who had never heard the name of Jesus, simply because there was no road to their village. Then He showed me the West, with its many millions of people choosing their own personal lifestyles rather than receiving Jesus as their Lord and Saviour.

I was still repeating, 'I am sorry, I am sorry.' After all, what could I do about it? And then I knew, even though I was only a girl, and said, 'Lord, I promise You that from this day on, and for the rest of my life, I will preach Your gospel everywhere that You send me. And I will encourage Your Church to do the same.'

I know that Father God accepted my promise for in the next second I was following Jesus up a steep hill and I was puffing to try and keep up with Him. As I followed Him, keeping my eyes fixed on His white garments, afraid to look left or right and keeping totally focused on Him, the path became narrower and steeper with more boulders to climb over on the way. I struggled even more to keep up, as Jesus walked so at ease in front of me.

We finally reached the top of the hill and Jesus sat down on a beautiful white marble rock and I panted, still tearful from my experience with the Father, and knelt down by His side. I had to take my eyes off Him in order to bow my head down onto the cold marble rock to worship, yet I knew He would not leave me so it was safe to do so.

As my head touched the white rock, I came out of the vision and my life totally changed. I had a mission ahead of me, given to me by the Father and Jesus. The road is getting steeper as the Ministry grows larger and as I keep my eyes focused on Jesus day and night, I know I will then keep up with Him and the work that He has for me to do. The other wonderful thing is that I know one day I will reach His side, and then, when I bow my head down on the white rock, I will not come out of the vision for this will be the end of my journey.

This was a vision, yet daily we can all come up into the Father's presence, for we can do nothing of ourselves. This is part of keeping our eyes on Jesus, for daily He will show us what to do, teach us what to say, and open our understanding more until we too can say truthfully, 'I can do nothing of myself but only what I see my Father doing, for whatever He does, I do likewise.'

This is my aim and I am putting this into practice more and more; and so can you. Once on the plane to India, I said, 'Lord, I am not going to do one thing this trip unless You show me, so, if You show me nothing, I will do nothing.' The Lord did not even wait for the plane to land before He spoke. 'You are not coming to India to preach or to teach, but to proclaim that the Kingdom of God is at hand. You are to prepare the people to receive from Me and I will do the rest.'

When I arrived, I found that my hosts could not speak English and I could not speak their language. Now I really had to wait on God, as to where we were going and the needs of the people and everything else. The Lord showed me every-thing: what to say, which people He was going to heal, even what they looked like in advance. The outcome was tremen-dous, for not even a moment was wasted. I connected with the people from the first sentence and the response was wonderful. After the sermon, I looked for the person whom the Lord had showed me in advance and invited her forward right up onto the platform and said to her, 'The Lord wants to heal you tonight. What would you like Him to do for you?' 'I would like to see; I have not been able to see anything for seven years.' 'In two minutes you will be able to see,' I told her and prayed over her eyes in Jesus' name. And within two minutes she is reading all the posters on the church walls. She is healed and all the people are rejoicing. 'This is the power of

Jesus at work in our midst,' I tell the people. 'Who would like
to receive this Jesus as Lord and Saviour?' Every hand goes up.
So I lead them through the sinner's prayer. And then I say, 'All
who are sick, lay your own hands on your sickness or pain and
the Lord will heal you now, and when you are healed put
your hand high in the air.' Within minutes, every hand has
gone up and we invite a few forward to testify before closing
the meeting and watching a very excited crowd leave, praising
their new found Lord and Saviour.

The Lord doesn't only allow us to see things concerning the
ministry that He has given us; He is just as interested in us
personally.

One evening, while in prayer, the Lord said to me, 'I want
to show you something.' I looked and the Lord showed me an
incident from a very long time ago and it took me a few
minutes to be able to connect that very familiar-looking tray
to when I was five years old. 'Oh yes, Lord, that was the first
thing I ever made at school for my mum and dad.' I
remembered sticking colourful pieces of paper that the
teacher had cut out to make a pattern on the tray. The
teacher then varnished it over and gave it me to take home.
That tray soon became old and tatty as the papers began to
peel through the varnish, as it was in our home for some
years. Suddenly the Lord said, 'I remember that too.' 'You
were there, Lord, and you remember that?' This was something that had happened before I even knew who Jesus was. I
had long forgotten it but He remembered! How could that be?
I was overwhelmed by His great love and suddenly realised
that every attempt, every effort to do something, even if no
one else sees, is noticed and remembered by our Lord. He
cares for us so much.

Seeing with your understanding is also very practical for
our everyday living. When I needed to do the plans for our
holiday farm, at a price that we could hopefully afford, I asked
the Lord to show us how to build it. Not only did He help me

to see what the building should look like, but He also showed me the size of every room, the height of the ceilings, the structure of the building and even how the drainage was to work. The building went up for less than a third of the price that had previously been quoted to us. About two years after the building had been in use, I was in Africa when my husband Wilfrid phoned me. 'There is a terrible leak coming through the ceiling of the disabled dormitory and we don't know where it is coming from; we will have to take the ceiling down to find out.' 'Don't do anything,' I replied. 'I will ask the Lord.' 'Please phone me soon though,' Wilfrid went on, 'as we have another camp coming on Friday.' I went into prayer and asked the Lord about the leak. After a little while, I saw in the spirit the U-bend just under the shower. I felt the Lord say, 'Remove the three tiles under the shower and you will see the leak.' I phoned Wilfrid and said, 'The Lord has shown me where the leak is. Just remove the three tiles in bathroom two and the leak is in the U-bend, directly under the shower.' Wilfrid went to do the job and found it exactly as I had told him. The whole job was done in about fifteen minutes.

These are a few of my experiences of living out the 'eyes of understanding' passage, but it goes far further than I have yet experienced. But any of us can have such experiences as we carry on our walk with Him.

Let us look at the time Jesus spent in God's presence, indicating how we should truly walk. In John 5:20 Jesus says,

> 'For the Father loveth the Son, and sheweth him all things that himself doeth: and he will shew him greater works than these, that ye may marvel.'

Here the Father speaks of greater works that He will do through His Son Jesus as a result of showing Him all things in prayer. Jesus, like us, had to build on His relationship with the

Father as well as grow from level to level in His works, as we
read in verse 21:

> *'For as the Father raiseth up the dead, and quickeneth them; even so
> the Son quickeneth whom he will.'*

Here He is speaking about us. Jesus will quicken whom He
will and that is you and me. Jesus also adds, concerning this
relationship,

> *'For the Father judgeth no man, but hath committed all judgment
> unto the Son: that all men should honour the Son, even as they
> honour the Father. He that honoureth not the Son honoureth not the
> Father which hath sent him.'*   (vv. 22–23)

Jesus became a man but He was also sent by God. In our
relationship in prayer, He will quicken us to do His work for
He says, in John 14:12,

> *'Verily, verily, I say unto you, he that believeth on me, the works
> that I do shall he do also; and greater works than these shall he do;
> because I go unto my Father.'*

Some questions to think about:

- How do the eyes of your understanding differ from the
  eyes in your head?
- How do we come into God's presence to understand
  this?
- How does seeing with your understanding help you to
  understand Scripture?
- How does seeing in the understanding help you in the
  practical?

How to Make Decisions in Prayer

'I can of mine own self do nothing: as I hear, I judge:
and my judgment is just; because I seek not mine own will,
but the will of the Father which hath sent me.'
(John 5:30)

Jesus did nothing of Himself because He was totally yielded to His Father, in complete joyful surrender to do His will and His will alone.

If Jesus did this, so must we. We need to die to our self-will and yield to God in that total joyful surrender, to hear Him and obey Him above our own desires. Then we will be able to say, like Jesus, in John 5:36,

> *'But I have greater witness than that of John: for the works which the Father hath given me to finish, the same works that I do, bear witness of me, that the Father hath sent me.'*

God sent Jesus into the world, but Jesus sends us to 'make disciples of all nations' and, in order that we do not hinder Him by our little minds (that is, in comparison to His), we need to be absolutely obedient. In verse 44 of this chapter,

Jesus asks, '*How can ye believe, which receive honour one of another, and seek not the honour that cometh from God only?*' We must please God, not man, obey God, not just man. We need to do only what God tells us to do.

Jesus' intimate and totally obedient relationship with His Father led to powerful and amazing results. In John 6:5–6 we read,

> '*When Jesus then lifted up his eyes, and saw a great company come unto him, he saith unto Philip, Whence shall we buy bread, that these may eat? And this he said to prove him: for he himself knew what he would do.*'

Then followed the wonderful miracle of feeding 5,000 people with five loaves and two fishes and the gathering up of no less than twelve baskets of leftovers. Jesus then departed to a mountain alone, after which He did another outstanding miracle, that of walking on the water. By now, multitudes were searching for Jesus and He explains the miracle in John 6:32–33,

> '*Then Jesus said unto them, Verily, verily, I say unto you, Moses gave you not that bread from heaven; but My Father giveth you the true bread from heaven. For the bread of God is he which cometh down from heaven, and giveth life unto the world.*'

Jesus is the bread of life who gives life to the world. Jesus came down from heaven to give life to the world, by doing the Father's will all the way to the cross. By dying on the cross, He won through, not only to the victory of rising from the dead, but also to complete victory over every sin, every sickness, every demon and over death. Then He ascended to heaven where He sits at the Father's right hand, above all rule and authority and above every name that is named.

We read in John 6:28–29,

'Then said they unto him, What shall we do, that we might work the works of God? Jesus answered and said unto them, This is the work of God, that ye believe on him whom he hath sent.'

And in John 4:33–35,

'Therefore said the disciples one to another, Hath any man brought him ought to eat? Jesus saith unto them, My meat is to do the will of Him that sent me, and to finish his work. Say not ye, There are yet four months, and then cometh harvest? behold, I say unto you, Lift up your eyes, and look on the fields; for they are white already to harvest.'

When we really believe Jesus, we will earnestly and sincerely want to do what He wants us to do and when we begin to do the works that He wants us to do, it is then that we begin to do the works of God. For God Himself will faithfully show us every time in prayer exactly what He wants us to do and we will begin to make right judgements and decisions, for we will be learning to make all those decisions in prayer. Firstly we must firmly resolve to do only what the Father tells us and that means spending time in prayer in order to hear what His will for us is and then obey Him. Secondly we must choose to make all our daily decisions in prayer and this means spending more time with God.

In 1974, as a new believer, I started Longfield Riding Centre in Port Elizabeth, South Africa, when it began to run at a loss. I sold a horse to pay the bills and carried on. The next month I still ran at a loss, and the next, and I had to sell another horse to pay the bills. I realised then that, if I sold any more horses, I would have insufficient with which to teach, so I came to the Lord with the problem. (This situation had come about largely due to not keeping up with inflation.)

I had given my life to the Lord about a year earlier, but now it dawned on me that it might be a good idea to give the Lord my business too, even in its poor state. The Lord received it, for He then proceeded to speak to me about finding another stable yard for my livery clients to take their horses. I was confused at such an instruction and said, 'Lord, I thought we were trying to build up the riding school by getting more people to board their horses, not to take their horses away to board elsewhere.' The Lord replied, 'Is it My riding school or your riding school?'

'Yours, Lord,' I replied.

This meant that I had to obey even though it did not make sense to me at the time. So I obeyed and my three clients who had their horses boarding with me reluctantly left. After this, some new pupils joined the school for riding lessons and the next month we did not make a loss and the following month we actually made a profit for the first time. It was then that I also had to have my books audited for the end of March tax. The auditor called me in and said, 'Take a look at this, see the fees that you are charging your boarders and compare them with your feed bill. You are undercharging your boarders and need to put the fees up a lot before you can think of making a profit.'

'I did not realise that the Lord knew about business management!' I blurted out. He looked at me stunned. I then told him what the Lord had told me to do in order to turn the riding school into a profitable business.

Since then, every decision I have made has been born in prayer and the outcome has always been success every time.

This lesson applies to decision-making both in the practical and the miraculous.

In the Transkei a few years later, we were part of a leadership team running a youth camp by the sea. As often happens in Africa, more children turned up than had booked and, as usual, we took them in. However, this made us short

Burma: Encouraging a family on Lake Inlay. They gave me my bonnet.

Burma: Morning market on Lake Inlay.

of food at the end of the camp, leaving only enough for one plate of breakfast cereal to be shared between seventeen leaders. The hostess did not know what to do, so she asked the Lord. The Lord said, 'Say grace as usual.' So she said grace, as we always do before meals, and she decided to give each of us one spoon each. Seeing more cereal still left, she carried on spooning and spooning until there were seventeen bowls full of cereal but there was still the same amount of cereal left in the packet! Only then did we realise that a miracle had happened.

Decision-making in prayer even works where things do not make sense, as long as we are obeying God's decision for that situation. My calling is to plant churches in remote villages but, through my book *Dare to Step Out in Faith*, I began to receive invitations to major cities, not to run crusades, but to simply speak in small churches. What was the Lord doing? How could I make any impact there? My only decision was to obey God and go. On 15th April, 2008, Barbara and I flew to New York. That night we stood by the Statue of Liberty looking across the river to the brilliantly lit city of New York.

As I stared at this massive city, I suddenly saw the vision again that the Lord had given me seventeen and a half years earlier on August 15th, 1990, just before going into the operating theatre to give birth to my daughter, Rebecca. Now I was seeing the fulfilment of that vision of bringing the Gospel to some of the major cities of the world and, since January 2008, I have spoken in Singapore, London, Hyderabad, Wellington and Christchurch. But there was more to it than this.

The New York pastor had been sharing with us on the way the impact *Dare to Step Out in Faith* had made on him and how he was trying to bring the power and authority of our living Jesus into his church and how this had led to difficulties and persecution from other churches. This is why I was invited. I had the challenge of bringing the reality of the living Jesus to some of New York's black churches. These were churches which were practising Christianity without power, with teachings in theory only, devoid of the reality. As a result, many were being tempted by the kind of power offered by the demonic and drug abuse is on the increase in the city.

When we were back in the car again, the pastor put on a Christian tape, 'Open the eyes of our hearts, Lord, we want to see Jesus . . .' Yes, I thought, open the eyes of our understanding Lord, we want to see from the heavenly realm. Isn't that what Ephesians means?

Oh, how God's heart cries out for this city of New York – the increasing sin, the drugs, the dabbling into demonic realms, in this fine city. We stopped and went into a clothing shop: T-shirts with skulls, skeletons, Buddhas . . . everything but Jesus! I remember thinking to myself, 'Yes, people are turning to the occult because the power of the cross has been removed from most of the churches and some churches have even been sold and turned into restaurants etc., just as in England. The churches need to wake up fast!'

When we returned to the pastor's home, I went to my room and asked the Lord, 'Lord, why did You bring me this vision of bringing Your message to major cities just before giving birth to Rebecca?' (Sometimes one has to kneel while waiting for the answer to such a question.) The Lord replied, 'You gave birth to a new life on that date which you will never forget. Rebecca you gave birth to in the physical, but now I want to use you to spark birth in the spiritual realm for revival. I am using you along with many others whom I have also called, to ignite a spark of revival which My pastors in each place will nurture into full maturity. Yes, and as you step forth with the same fear and trembling as before you gave birth physically – knowing that the pain of childbirth was just ahead of you – in the same way step out boldly as you did then, knowing that there is no other way but to walk forward into it. Yes, and in the same way, similar pains will lie ahead

but so will the joy abound when your work has been
completed in Me.'

I suddenly realised that a vision that the Lord had given me
seventeen and a half years ago had only now become reality
and saw with a new insight how exact the Lord is and what
lengths He will go to, to teach a person.

I then remembered a phone call from a man who wanted
the answer as to why Abraham should lie in Genesis 12:13. I
remembered the answer to that question from a course I had
gone on some years ago on the Eblo archaeological finds,
from a Rabbi. God did not ask Abraham to lie, but rather
the Scriptures were kept so accurate in detail to reveal to
us today how true every word of the Bible is. Only in the
1980s the archaeologists discovered that there were actually
two marriage contracts in that era, the first being similar to
the marriage contracts we have today, the second being the
sister contract that meant that the marriage could never be
separated by divorce or by any other means.

Telling Pharaoh that Sarah was married with the sister
contract was to protect Sarah from Pharaoh, for Pharaoh
could not touch any woman married with the sister contract.

How we need to thank every person who wrote our Bibles
that even when the words did not make sense at the time,
they made the right decision to keep every word of Sripture
accurate so that the Lord could use even more proof of
Scripture to bring yet another person to Himself.

Some questions to think about:

- Why should we make decisions in prayer?
- How do we make decisions in prayer?
- What results from decisions made in prayer?
- How will this affect your life?

How to Submit to the Lord

4

'For I came down from heaven, not to do mine own will,
but the will of him that sent me.'
(John 6:38)

Submitting to the Lord is probably the hardest thing for us to do, for the flesh is always fighting the spirit and wants its own way. It is harder than making a decision in prayer, for we seek an answer there. Now we have to go a step further to see our lives not for what we want, but rather as doing the will of the Lord.

If we read how Jesus was tested, it makes it even harder, for John 6: 39–41 goes on to say,

> *'And this is the Father's will which hath sent me, that of all which he hath given me I should lose nothing, but should raise it up again at the last day. And this is the will of him that sent me, that every one which seeth the Son, and believeth on him, may have everlasting life: and I will raise him up at the last day. The Jews then murmured at him, because he said, I am the bread which came down from heaven.'*

But Jesus knew what the Father wanted Him to say and, despite opposition, verse 53 continues,

'Then Jesus said unto them, Verily, verily, I say unto you, Except ye eat the flesh of the Son of man, and drink his blood, ye have no life in you.'

Read on. The disciples fell away and even Jesus' own brothers disbelieved Him. Chapter 7:1 records,

'After these things Jesus walked in Galilee: for he would not walk in Jewry, because the Jews sought to kill him.'

How many of us are prepared to do the Father's will, even in the face of opposition? If Jesus had disobeyed the Father to save Himself from being killed by the Jews, He would not have been able to teach us the truth and to prepare us to receive the greatest gift the world could ever receive through His death and resurrection on the third day. We simply have to die to our own will, in order to do the will of Him who gave His life for us. Sometimes this is not easy.

An invitation to Pakistan turned out to be at the time of the Danish newspaper Muslim cartoon strikes and everyone advised that it would be very unwise to go at this dangerous time, but I felt it was God's will for me to go – that is, until I arrived at the airport. I went in and out of the line three times before I heard the Lord say, 'I have called you and will not forsake you.' After that, I was able to obey and continue on. Burma was another difficult invitation, as preaching in Burma is against the law and I was invited to speak at four pastors' seminars in four different states. I did not want to go. I really didn't but I managed to find someone to come with me. Once we were there, we could virtually feel the oppression the people were under and were in constant fear of being arrested. But whenever fears of being arrested for preaching to the congregation entered my mind, I just prayed for courage and was able to preach boldly.

When we entered the second state, a massive Buddhist

festival was taking place and we felt led to spend part of the first evening at the festival watching the great paper balloons going up into the sky and tasting some of the sweet cakes. The next day was spent teaching at the pastors' conference. We arrived back at the hotel to find that the authorities had been there three times to look for us, but the receptionist had told them that we had gone to the Buddhist festival and that we had been seen walking there the night before.

Up in my room, I gathered together my itinerary and headed paper and washed them under the tap before flushing them down the toilet, in case we were searched. 'Lord, I exclaimed, I haven't the nerve to do this work.' We then booked out of the hotel and caught a taxi to Lake Inle and had to change taxis as the first one lost a wheel. We arrived in time to see the traditional horse traps and have a walk round the village.

Next morning we were up at 5 a.m. to encourage a Christian family on the islands of Lake Inle. We sped through the waters by motorised canoe with the sunrise coming over the misted hills. Soon we were at the islands where we saw a sinking temple and people with extremely long necks. On part of the island the canoe market was already becoming busy with fruit, vegetables and other produce. We then sped on to the next village and the next. We met the pastors' friends, encouraged them and were back by 9 a.m. Someone had given me a Shan bonnet and I had bought a colourful Shan hat very cheaply. After that, we caught a taxi back to town to complete the pastors' seminar.

On arriving back in town, I got out of the taxi and pulled out my rucksack to put it on my back and walk the rest of the way. Not having anywhere to put my Shan hat, I put it on my head over the bonnet in order to get my arm through the other side of my rucksack. Seeing an official approach me, I burst out laughing, realising how funny I must look wearing two hats! At that, the official suddenly turned round and walked off and we went on our way. As we went, I heard the familiar small still voice say, 'Yes, you do *not* have the nerve to do this work. That is why I gave you *My* nerves of steel.' I was then told that the official who had walked away was the man trying to find me, but I probably looked more like a crazy tourist than a speaker so he must have decided that I was not the right person!

When we submit to not doing our own will but our Father's will, He will lead us and protect us. Sometimes people ask me, 'How do you know God's will, how do you hear Him?' The Lord tries to speak to us all the time. But often we are so busy that we do not give Him the time to speak to us or guide us. Then we get into the danger of walking in the flesh and doing what we think is right instead of walking in obedience according to what we have heard the Lord say to us.

I would like to share some insights from what the Lord taught me in the mountains of New Zealand. It is good to draw aside alone with Him sometimes and wait for Him to speak to us. First of all it was the Lord who told me to accept the invitation to New Zealand, to speak in some churches in both the South and North Islands. He then gave me a serious message of warning for the churches to unite and stand firm against the ungodly influences that were penetrating their country from other countries. I was amazed at how well they received this message and how the church immediately took action in response to it.

I also managed to find three days to go into the mountains and the Lord spoke to me about many things. The first day I climbed Mount John above Lake Tekapo. At the very top, I sat down on a rock overlooking lakes and snow-capped mountains in the wind, to wait on the Lord. He immediately began to speak to me. 'Tune into Me directly or My voice may come to you muffled, just as the wind blows about your ears when side-on as you are now. Now look straight into the wind. Now you can hear the wind clearly, you can hear with both ears and not just one. In the same way, I need your time and full concentration. It is a great responsibility to hear Me right and to declare what I give you with accuracy. Keep finely in tune with My Holy Spirit with both ears open, facing Me full on. If you do this, you will hear Me clearly and you will not limit Me.' Later, down on the lake, He showed me the gentle ripples and said, 'In yielded stillness, the waters yield to the breeze that blows them to the shore ripple by ripple. Do not think in your heart that what you do for Me is of small account. No, My child, for every ripple is important and, as My children obey Me, the many ripples will cause their own ripple effect, until there are so many that the ripples will intermingle and cause a tide of My revival.'

The next day I visited Mount Cook and waited patiently for the clouds to lift so that I could take a photograph. This took some waiting and the Lord said, 'I too like My people to wait on Me, as this stills their minds and brings them into the same sense of expectancy as you wait for Mount Cook to reveal its beauty. So too I will reveal My beauty to those who wait on Me. And as My people search their hearts, so the clouds of oppression or conflict or difficulties loose themselves from their hearts as the clouds begin to lift that hide My presence from them. Even so, as you watch the rainclouds begin to lift, so Mount Cook will be seen in all its beauty and splendour. That is how I too wish to reveal Myself to My people who wait on Me.'

Within a few minutes, Mount Cook did reveal itself, with bright sunlight shining on its snow caps against a brilliant blue sky. I took my photographs and marvelled at such beauty. It is a sight like this that inspires one to feel that this is where the earth touches the skies and where heaven touches earth, separated only by occasional clouds. It seemed to me in the same way that the earthly realm touches the spiritual but the heavenly realm is often hidden by the clouds of sin, oppression, pain or sickness in people's lives. The Lord then said, 'I call My chosen ones to get rid of every cloud in their lives and to rise up in Me above the clouds into the heavenly realm where I ask each one to live in My presence. It is then that heaven will invade your souls, transform your minds, and cause you to rise up above every care and every problem, for you will see My answer, not only for your own life, but you will also be able to take My answer to this hurting, troubled world, to bring release, salvation, healing and deliverance to many. Prayer will become your life source and the things of heaven will be within your grasp.' Slowly the magnificent sun-drenched picture of Mount Cook was again being covered by cloud and hidden completely from view. 'So with me,' the Lord continued, 'I will occasionally give you a glimpse of My power and My glory, of My majestic splendour to encourage you, but most often you must walk the path of faith, knowing that I am still there, just as sure as Mount Cook is hidden behind clouds. And so the clouds of problems, sickness, hurt and sin still invade the earth. Rise up above them all into the sunlight of My presence and then you will be able to bring My message of love and salvation to all, near and far, and, as you do, I will use the clouds that brought problems to My people, even as storms do to nature, to water and germinate new life as they turn to Me, their Saviour.'

Later, after I returned to where I was staying, I went for a walk in the wind and the Lord spoke again. 'See the mountains. Some are under an open heaven in purest sunlight and others are under storm clouds, so it is with My cities and so many areas or villages you are to minister in. You need to look at these cities or villages in the Spirit realm and I will reveal to you the strongholds over them. And you are to pray them down and release My people from those oppressions, until I put an open heaven above these places. I will then send you in to a responsive people. The strongholds are many that can oppress a city, village or area. These keep people in bondage so that they are unable to hear or respond to any message given. These strongholds are to be prayed down first, wherever My people are to preach and this has to be taken seriously so that no time is lost. Binding these strongholds can be done in serious, effective prayer before your meeting. This will bind down the strongholds for the duration of the meeting. For whole cities, it may take a whole group of intercessors up to a year on a weekly basis. Every situation is different so My people must seek Me for each strategy for that area. Yes, I am calling My people to a serious commitment, a new alertness and to move only in Me. I desire that My people take command in Me in the spirit realm. When they learn to take command, then My work will be accomplished. When you intercede for another person, do not *only* pray for the negative things in their life to leave in My name but also pray for My love, My peace, My joy, My strength to uplift them in Jesus' name. See the great lakes that have formed from the glaciers. Do you think that My lakes of blessings are not as large? The resources from heaven are almost untapped. As I require you to pray off the strongholds that hold My people in bondage, so I also require you to release the blessings from heaven. Whatever you bind on earth is bound in heaven and whatever you release unto earth is released from heaven. I want My people to pray these things into reality. I am grieved at half-hearted prayer. Unless My people pray with their whole heart, how can they expect Me to answer? I call for true belief in Me and wholehearted prayer. Then My people will see Me answer their prayer. I look at the heart and half-hearted, lukewarm people I spit out. I am looking for My real people who will worship with *all* their hearts and seek My face in reality and truth. These are My real people and I am calling them together now. I want to raise them up. I have a call on such people's lives. I want to use them to extend My kingdom and I want to bless them abundantly.

'So you think in your heart that you have never heard Me speak so much. Have you given Me the time? Do My people give Me the time to speak to them and teach them? No, they just go their own way. That is why My world is in such a state. Yes, My children, I want you to reorganise your lifestyles and priorities so that you can hear Me speak to you, then I will send you the help you need. No longer must you allow over-busy lives to steal your time with Me. Praying on the run or through the night is not what I require, for then you are too rushed to hear My voice. I wish for you to live a life of prayer-balance, not make-up time. Do you realise that the devil will go to great lengths to make My people busy? This is so that he can steal from you your greatest asset: your time of prayer with Me. Even the reading of My Word has been rushed and this I cannot tolerate. Return fully to Me, My beloved children, and I will meet with you. Then you will see what I will do and you will be amazed. Rise up, put your hand firmly in Mine and we shall walk together.'

On Friday morning I walked down to the Shepherd's Chapel but it was closed because of the rain and the Lord spoke again. 'Yes, My child, the times are closing down. More and more churches will close their doors, more and more ungodly things will overtake this earth, for Satan is waging his last battle and then the end will come to this present age.

'I call My people to prayer, serious, serious prayer, that you may be overcomers. Yes, My child, time is very, very short. Do not think in your mind, "Where shall I escape to?" For those who try and save their life shall lose it but those who lose their life for My sake and My gospel shall find it. Rather concentrate your eyes on Me and keep your ears focused on My counsel and guidance. Those who seek Me will find Me and those who listen will hear My voice. Do you realise that today's satellites can already trace every human being, even if they are in the remotest jungle or mountain range? But do not despair that you cannot hide from the enemy but rather rejoice that, through My Holy Spirit who dwells in your heart, *nothing* can separate you from Me. My Holy Spirit is far greater than any scientific invention ever made. My Holy Spirit connects up to Me every human being who has received Me as Lord and, through this, they can rise above the coming disasters through prayer until they are raptured right into My very heaven. Know, My child, that your spirit and soul are worth exceedingly more than your flesh. The world can only attack the flesh, but the devil is after your soul as well and this you need to guard at all costs. Hold dear to the Holy Spirit I have placed in your heart and you will be saved. Think not in your heart that the mark of the beast to come is only psychological and of small significance. No, My child, the very receiving of that mark will require your *soul*, your *mind* and your *will*, causing you to be lost forever from the kingdom of heaven. The choice is, either you believe Me, or you do not. If you believe Me, you will never accept the mark but will rise up in Me, in the power of My Holy Spirit within you, to the glory of My kingdom.'

I have shared with you this message which I heard from the Lord in those beautiful mountains in New Zealand for I believe that these words were not for me alone but for others too.

The Lord does speak to us and, as we endeavour to do only the Father's will, He will speak to us more and more and guide us every step of the way, just as He did for Jesus, until we can say like Jesus, 'I am here on earth not to do My own will but the will of the Father.'

It is not just a matter of serving God but rather serving God from within His presence, in joyful surrendered obedience, born out of a close relationship with Him, seeing with Him your course of action, knowing He is with you and that He will do what you cannot do. This type of service is more in 'teamwork' with the Lord. It is fully effective and results in much fruit. Working from within His presence is much more effective than working *for* Him. It is only in prayer that we discover this and then live it out in action.

Each saying of Jesus on 'only doing the Father's will' teaches us not only to fully depend on 'only doing the Father's will' but also indicates the different areas that this will affect in our lives and ultimately raise us up into a new level of walking in Him.

The more we come to know God, the more we will know how to walk in Him, as we serve Him in the ministries which He has entrusted to us.

Some questions to think about:

- Why is it important to submit to the Lord?
- What would submitting to God result in our life?
- Why is it important to give the Lord time to speak to us?
- How does this affect your life?

New Zealand: Wendy had an injured lower back for many years causing sciatica and jerking of legs. When she forgave herself she was instantly healed and is now able to touch her toes.

How to Plan in Prayer and Prepare Sermons

5

*'Jesus answered them, and said, my doctrine is not
mine, but his that sent me. If any man will do his will,
he shall know of the doctrine, whether it be of God,
or whether I speak of myself. He that speaketh
of himself seeketh his own glory: but he that seeketh
his glory that sent him, the same is true,
and no unrighteousness is in him.'*
(John 7:16–18)

In the last chapter we spoke of 'only doing the Father's will' and how the Lord reveals His will to us in a more general way. This chapter will deal with coming into His presence for a specific purpose such as a sermon.

This verse 18 of John 7 took on a new meaning while visiting Kampala in Uganda in September 2008. The Lord had shown me how I was to speak on the three gifts of 'salvation, righteousness and the Holy Spirit' over and over again. I was to show how the gift of salvation delivered us from sin through repentance and receiving Jesus as Lord and Saviour. But at this level the devil could still tempt us and we had to fight sin to walk closer to Christ. Then there was the gift of righteousness described in Romans 5:17–21,

'For if by one man's offence death reigned by one; much more they which receive abundance of grace and of the gift of righteousness shall reign in life by one, Jesus Christ. Therefore as by the offence of one judgment came upon all men to condemnation; even so by the righteousness of one the free gift came upon all men unto justification of life. For as by one man's disobedience many were made sinners, so by the obedience of one shall many be made righteous. Moreover the law entered, that the offence might abound. But where sin abounded, grace did much more abound: That as sin hath reigned unto death, even so might grace reign through righteousness unto eternal life by Jesus Christ our Lord.'

The devil has no regard for a sinner as he has control over that person already and knows that the wages of sin is death. But the devil fears the righteous man.

Sin causes man to become weaker and weaker. For instance, when does an alcoholic become an alcoholic? It is the moment when the lure of alcohol becomes stronger than the person's ability to say 'no' – the person will get less and less able to say 'no' to temptation, until they are the prisoner of the demons themselves who will torment them in hell.

But Jesus has given us all a way out: true repentance that leads to salvation, righteousness and eternal life. We have free will after receiving the free gift of salvation. Paul stresses how we must do *our* part to continually *choose* to receive the gift of righteousness in 1 Timothy 6:11,

'But thou, O man of God, flee these things; and follow after righteousness, godliness, faith, love, patience, meekness.'

Elsewhere Paul speaks of it in Romans 10:10,

'For with the heart man believeth unto righteousness; and with the mouth confession is made unto salvation.'

Jesus' brother James talks of righteousness in James 5:16,

> *'Confess your faults one to another, and pray one for another, that ye may be healed. The effectual fervent prayer of a righteous man availeth much.'*

Just as a sinner becomes weaker and weaker through sin, so the man who pursues righteousness, who is able to say 'no' to sin and 'yes' to God, becomes stronger and stronger in righteousness until the gift of righteousness frees us from sin. When we submit to God to do only His will, there will be no unrighteousness in us. How wonderful this word of God is. One man asked me, 'If the gift of righteousness is a free gift, why must we work towards it?' But if you were given a plane, would you fly it? No, you would need many lessons! Similarly the Bible teaches and trains us in all righteousness. You need fuel for the plane to take off and air to hold it up. In the same way, prayer with righteousness and the wind of the Holy Spirit will enable us to take off and stay up there in the higher dimensions of faith.

The gift of the Holy Spirit and the nine supernatural gifts enable us to walk by faith and, like the plane, we move forward in obedience to do exactly what the Father has told us to do.

This message had far-reaching effects at the International Youth Conference, then at the Leaders' Summit 2008 and after that at various other ministries and churches. It was at a large church on the second weekend of my Uganda trip that I also preached this message and led the whole congregation through the prayer of repentance and thought it was complete. So I led the congregation through the next stage of entering the presence of God through prayer and invited the Holy Spirit gifts to operate. Suddenly an elderly man stood up and repeated, 'Repent, repent . . .' seven times. One by one, we all knelt down in response and, this time, everyone repented in tears. Now the Holy Spirit really came down and began to free the people and bring inner healing and physical healing. I then said, 'There is someone struggling with unforgiveness' and, all of a sudden, there was a scream and a paralysed woman slithering forward on the floor, crying out, 'I will never forgive my sister! I would rather die than forgive my sister.'

The next day I met Godfrey, an evangelist, and he had arranged what looked like a crusade for unbelievers in his garden. So I gave the same message again and called people to come forward to receive salvation. No one came forward. So I asked those who wished to be baptized in the Holy Spirit to come forward. Again no one came forward. I then asked, 'Does anyone wish to seriously pursue the gift of righteousness?' The entire audience came forward and the Holy Spirit came down and I prayed for each one as they cried. I was then told that they were all pastors!

We then left to go home. We stopped at the church where I had spoken the day before and dropped off the bishop's daughter. I spotted the paralysed woman there and asked the bishop if I could pray for her. I quickly set up my camera in anticipation of a miracle and then approached her. I said that the Lord would heal her if she would forgive her sister for not letting her go to the USA with her. She agreed to forgive her and we prayed the prayer of forgiveness. All of a sudden, her paralysed leg began to shake and she said she felt power come into it. Then she was able to bend her knee and she got up and began to walk for the first time in thirteen months!

On the way home Godfrey said how my old-time message on sin and righteousness was the right message for Kampala at this hour. Revival had come to Uganda after the Idi Amin era and many miracles had happened. But during the last few years, the prosperity message had come in and many pastors had left the message of repentance to one side, and taken their eyes off the spiritual blessings of God for the message of prosperity, looking to material blessings of cars and houses instead. Sin had crept into many of their lives. Now this message was causing them to return to the true biblical gospel where real miracles happen as they had just seen. He also mentioned the importance of the simple gospel message I had preached to the pastors that night and the true repentance they had come to.

Godfrey brought home to me my actual theological standing of sticking to the true gospel of salvation, righteousness and gifts of the Holy Spirit that leads to genuine manifestations of healings and miracles following.

All I had done was obey the Lord and give the message He had given me to preach, not realising all that God would do through it. How I praise the Lord for doing yet again *far* more than I could ever think or imagine through simple obedience. For this is truly God's work and His way of working.

John 7:28–29 goes on to say,

> *'Then cried Jesus in the temple as he taught, saying, Ye both know me, and ye know whence I am: and I am not come of myself, but he that sent me is true, whom ye know not. But I know him: for I am from him, and he hath sent me.'*

In verses 33–34 Jesus then said to them,

> *'Yet a little while am I with you, and then I go unto him that sent me. Ye shall seek me, and shall not find me: and where I am, thither ye cannot come.'*

Here He was speaking of His body which, after He was raised from the dead, would ascend to heaven to the right hand of God. In John 7:37–39 we read,

> *'In the last day, that great day of the feast, Jesus stood and cried, saying, If any man thirst, let him come unto me, and drink. He that*

believeth on Me, as the scripture hath said, out of his belly shall flow rivers of living water. (But this spake he of the Spirit, which they that believe on him should receive: for the Holy Ghost was not yet given; because that Jesus was not yet glorified.)'

Here, Jesus was speaking about the spirit realm. We cannot go in our body to where Jesus is, but we can go there in the Spirit through prayer. As we come into His presence to wait on Him in the spiritual realm in prayer, He will speak to us powerfully so that out of our bodies will flow rivers of living water. Waiting on God is not being passive but is born of a passion to do His will. It is waiting on God as to *how* to do it. Our love for God takes us into the discipline of waiting to find out how to express love creatively and effectively in His service. Without this discipline and focus, we run the risk of not hearing God in some instances and this could cause problems to arise. Through waiting on God with this intense focus, He will answer and equip us for the work ahead.

If we try to make up a sermon from our own limited knowledge, regardless of how much training we may have had or how well we speak, and if we do it in our own strength, then the Lord will say, 'Well, you don't need Me then.' And He will leave that person with little or no fruit to follow. No signs or healings will follow a person who only speaks what they have put together, but when a person hears God for their sermon, it does not matter whether they are a good speaker or not for they speak the words of God. God Himself will honour His word with signs and wonders and healings that will follow such a sermon.

It does not matter if your pastor has given you only a few minutes to speak, for God can work around that. As you bring the scriptures that you have been given before God, and ask Him how to put together a sermon from them, He will show you and He will bring wonderful promptings to your mind and bring excitement to your spirit. You will be able to take hold of the revelation that Jesus is showing you and He will give you an authority in Him to preach with power and meaning. Revelations that you receive from God are exciting to share. Your authority in preaching that sermon will show because you know that they are God's words and not your own. When you preach God's word God's way, an expectancy fills your heart and the words are carried over to the people with feeling, with meaning and with urgency and the people will respond because they recognise the word as being from God. It is wonderful to preach God's word like that and, as you get into the flow with the Lord, your faith begins to rise in expectancy of the healings that you know will follow. A couple of times, my faith has risen so much that I ask for the sickest person to be brought forward *first* so that everyone can watch Jesus heal the person. And the Lord does heal that person and the people's faith is raised to a new level and a charged atmosphere for healings seems to follow as many receive their healings from the Lord. On some occasions, I have even had the privilege of seeing every single person healed by Jesus, and that is how it should be. Every sermon that Jesus preached was received from the Father, which is why they were perfect. Jesus lived in a perfect relationship with His Father and only spoke that which the Father gave Him to speak.

Jesus also planned in prayer as we see in John 8:4–5,

> *'They say unto him, Master, this woman was taken in adultery, in the very act. Now Moses in the law commanded us, that such should be stoned: but what sayest thou?'*

Let us see how Jesus reacted. He did not rush into a reply but stooped down and wrote something with His finger as though He hadn't heard them. I believe that at this point Jesus was asking God how He should answer them. Jesus knew that they were trying to accuse Him and needed a plan

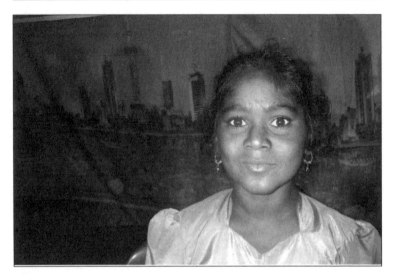

India: Suzanne calls up the sickest person. They send up Pattem Bayamma born deaf and dumb and Jesus heals her completely. She can now repeat sentences after Suzanne. As a result over 2,000 receive Jesus as Lord.

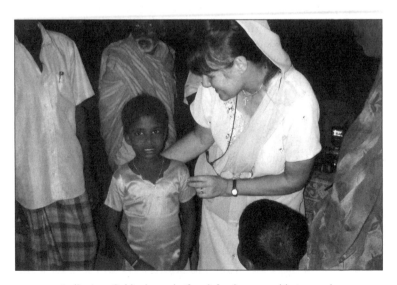

India: Jaya Subha born deaf and dumb – now able to speak.

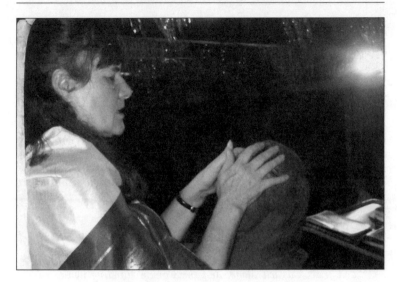

India: Therasa, blind for 5 years, was shown to Suzanne before the meeting.
Suzanne called her up and the Lord instantly healed her.
This healing was shown on India TV news that evening.

'Who would like to receive Jesus as Lord?'
All 160,000 jumped up to receive!

of wisdom to outwit them and this God gave Him as we read next:

> 'So when they continued asking him, he lifted up himself, and said unto them, he that is without sin among you, let him first cast a stone at her. And again he stooped down, and wrote on the ground.'
>
> (vv. 7–8)

Was He now waiting on God to convict the men around Him of their sin? Let us see what happens next.

> And they which heard it, being convicted by their own conscience, went out one by one, beginning at the eldest, even unto the last: and Jesus was left alone, and the woman standing in the midst. When Jesus had lifted up himself, and saw none but the woman, he said unto her, Woman, where are those thine accusers? hath no man condemned thee? She said, No man, Lord. And Jesus said unto her, Neither do I condemn thee: go, and sin no more.'
>
> (vv. 9–11)

Why is this story of the adulterous woman told in Scripture in such detail? I believe everything recorded in Scripture is for our benefit to instruct us about how we should live. If we came to Jesus for every answer, as Jesus came to His father, just think of the wisdom God would give to us! Just think of the excellent planning He would reveal to us for our lives. Just think of the wonderful sermons He would give us to preach. Just think of the results that would be achieved.

I would now like to share one experience of hearing God and saying only what He told me in my own life.

In India in November 2007 I had to speak at a crusade of over 2,000 Hindu people and the Lord showed me exactly what to say. This took some boldness to obey as it was in the middle of a Hindu festival. 'How should I share this?' I asked Him. 'By questions,' He replied.

I began by saying, 'I see that you are a very religious people and have thousands of gods. But I see one thing in common with all of them. I see that every god represents something from this earth, an animal or reptile or nature. Is that right?' They all agreed that it was right. 'Would you like to hear about the one and only God in heaven?' I asked. And they all shouted, 'Yes!' I shared with them how God so loved the world that He sent His only Son Jesus from heaven and how He died on the cross to pay the price for our sins. And then how three days later He rose in complete victory over every sin, every sickness and every demon and ascended back to heaven where He sits at the right hand of the Father who has sent His Holy Spirit to dwell in every heart that receives Jesus as Lord and Saviour. I then told them that in Genesis, it is written that God created us in His own image and I asked, 'Would any of you like to be created in the image of any god in this world?' They looked at me in horror and shouted, 'No, no, no!' And I said, 'Are you happy that you are created in the same image as God in heaven?' They all shouted, 'Yes!' and began to jump up and down as their eyes were opened as to who they really are, humans created in the image of the God of heaven. By now, my own faith had risen to a new level and I asked them to bring a very sick person. They brought a girl, born deaf and dumb. I prayed for her and, within two minutes, she could repeat sentences in English after me. 'This is the power of Jesus at work!' I shouted. 'This is because Jesus is alive. Who wants to receive this Jesus as Lord and Saviour?' Over 2,000 hands shot up and I led them through the sinner's prayer. They were jumping up and down and wanting me to lay hands on them and to pray that they would follow Jesus faithfully for the rest of their lives. 'Lord', I prayed, 'what do I do now? There are too many to pray for.' Suddenly I knew I had heard God: I called all the evangelists to form a 'prayer tunnel', so that as the people went through the tunnel they would all receive prayer. Then something unexpected happened. Those who had demons were unable to go into the tunnel because, as the demons began to manifest themselves, people were thrown onto the ground. So a few of us cast out the demons which went quite quickly and, as soon as the demons left them, the people were able to go through the prayer tunnel. It was amazing how terrified the demons were of the prayer tunnel. I then told the sick to lay hands on their own sicknesses or pain and receive healing in Jesus' Name and to put their hands up when they had received their healing. After a few minutes, hundreds of hands went up and some came forward to give their testimonies of their healings. The Lord had done it again! He had come down to save, heal and deliver over 2,000 people. When we do as God tells us, He gives us the message, He gives us the wisdom and He Himself confirms it with His miracles of healing and deliverance. *Jesus is Lord and He is doing it!*

Some questions to think about:

- How does planning in prayer affect our sermons or walk?
- How does obedience produce signs and wonders to follow?
- Give an example in the life of Jesus.
- Give an example from your own life or how you wish to respond.

How to Discern What Is from God

> 'Ye judge after the flesh; I judge no man. And yet if I judge,
> my judgment is true: for I am not alone,
> but I and the Father that sent me.
> (John 8:15–16)

We read in John 8:17–18,

> 'It is also written in your law, that the testimony of two men is true.
> I am one that bear witness of myself, and the Father that sent me
> beareth witness of me.'

We also have the Word of God as well as hearing His voice and when both of these line up with each other in agreement, we will know what is from God and what is from the flesh and what is from the devil.

It is very important to ask the Lord for help when we have to decide who to trust and who *not* to trust, to discern properly which person is from God or speaking from God. This is also essential in the use of prophecy. Jesus knows who are His and who are not His but we can be fooled. People can pretend to be Christians so that we give them a paid job. I receive many invitations and many requests for help when I am in Africa or India. I have to come to God for help, to know the genuine needs from those who are trying to use us for their own ends. Often I have to go into their areas to check their work. I have to be alert to every deceptive scheme. I also have to guard our work so that every pastor stays true to his calling and the Lord gives me various ways to check this. I have to honour the people who give to this ministry so that every penny given is used in the right way. I go to great lengths to ensure my bookkeeping is thorough, and double-check that for each bicycle given there is a record of the person who hands it over witnessed by a signature from the evangelist who receives a bicycle, complete with photos.

In John 8:26 Jesus says:

> *'I have many things to say and to judge of you: but he that sent me is true; and I speak to the world those things which I have heard of him.'*

If we bring every single area that needs discernment or judgment to His hands, the Lord will show us every time, what or who is of God, what or who is of the flesh and what or who is of the devil. Prayer is vital if we are going to save time, difficulties and money. We have to ask God every time.

In countries closed to the Gospel, discernment is of the utmost importance and it is here that I have met the strongest Christians, for they know how important it is to abide in the Lord's presence and stay connected to Him in every situation. They need to know from the Lord when and to whom they should witness, and when they must not. They need to discern who they will invite to church services, which way to walk to church, when to make a detour or change plans altogether, as they discern that they are being followed. When people stay constantly in tune with the Lord, they know that they are not alone and that the Lord is with them, helping and guiding them all the way.

Discernment is also necessary when praying for someone to be healed who is not responding. We need to discern the underlying cause of the sickness. In New Zealand, I prayed for someone with arthritis and she came to me after the service to say that she was still in terrible pain and that she was the only one not healed and wanted to know why. I immediately asked the Lord for discernment and the word 'unforgiveness' came into my head. I asked her if she had a problem with unforgiveness and she burst into tears and said she could never forgive herself for what she had done. I told her Jesus was waiting to forgive her and heal her but only if she could forgive herself. After a while I persuaded her to make the decision to forgive herself and I led her through a prayer. As soon as she had forgiven herself and accepted the Lord's forgiveness, all the pain left and her tears turned into tears of joy as she was completely set free.

I was invited to speak in a city in America. The pastor moved in the prophetic and I discerned that what he prophesied to each person was not from God but was a way to collect a bigger offering. I had to hear from God with discernment as to how to warn the pastor of this error, so that he would gracefully receive the correction and turn to God and hear Him instead. He did receive the correction, resulting to new growth in his church.

At other times we have to use discernment in going to the most remote and hard-to-reach places with a person we have not met before and know nothing about, and at the same time be adequately prepared for the completely unknown. I had such an experience in Haiti where it was the other way round. I was a bit suspicious, especially when the pastor and his colleague were an hour late collecting me, and secondly I was travelling alone, yet I did feel that the Lord had sent me.

Soon we were travelling over mountain ranges in a four-wheel drive vehicle, along donkey tracks and very rough roads. Ten hours later we descended into Pillay which looked like a Wild-West town, but, instead of horses, donkeys were tied up outside the buildings.

We turned towards a very wide river, the car stopped and the two men got out. After five minutes they were back in the vehicle and, to my horror, began to drive straight through the river, with the tide pushing the car sideways towards the sea. That alone made me pray overtime!

We did make it across the river and up another mountain pass where the road was non-existent. It took a lot of turning and reversing and driving forward again to get round the sharp mountain donkey tracks, with long drops over the edges of the cliffs! Soon we could go no further so we left the vehicle and walked, carrying our luggage. By this time it was getting dark and we still had two canyons to climb through.

An hour later we reached an open-thatched church full of people and I was asked if I would like to preach straightaway or have fifteen minutes to change. I was led to a mud-built building and shown to a small dark room with shutters for windows. I quickly changed with the aid of my torch and walked back to the church to preach.

After I preached, I called the sick forward and began to lay hands on them. They were not having that and they rejected my laying hands on them. So I stopped the meeting, saying I was tired and returned to my room in the hut, totally confused and hearing arguing in the background from the church. I called out to God, 'Lord, what have I done wrong?'

The Lord showed me that I was in voodoo country. Haiti is the heart of voodoo and I was the first white person to come into this area. The voodoo priests would literally blow their curses wherever they wanted. They did *not* lay hands on people. These people had come to see if Christianity was better than voodoo. They were looking for a God who was more powerful than voodoo and the laying on of hands did not impress them. 'Lord, what do I do?' The Lord replied, 'Preach My Gospel.' For the next three days, I preached the Gospel, the power of the cross, what Jesus had done for us, who we are in Christ, the gift of righteousness, and proclaimed that the Kingdom of God was at hand.

On the last day, I issued a challenge to them and some of them received Jesus as Lord, but I had not yet prayed for any sick people. So I asked if any were sick to raise their hands. Nobody put a hand up. Then a woman came forward and took the microphone and said, 'I was healed the moment I received Jesus as Lord and Saviour.' Another came and said, 'I was healed through hearing the Word of God.' Others followed and shared the same thing. Every sick person was healed, simply through hearing or responding to the Gospel message. Many more then received Jesus as Lord. Suddenly all of them stood up and began to praise their new-found Lord and Saviour in the most ecstatic joy I have ever experienced.

God had revealed to them that He really was the true God, far more powerful than voodoo and He had healed them all without any laying on of hands, without any words from me, but simply through their hearing the Gospel. The Lord had done it yet again.

The reason I have shared this story is because the fear of going into such a remote place over very difficult terrain had made it hard to discern God's will clearly, but the fear drove me even more earnestly into prayer to hear *His* discernment and strategy. As I obeyed, the Lord Himself moved power-fully, surprising me yet again at the way He comes into our midst and does far, far more than we ever expect.

Some questions to think about

- How does John 8:15–16 challenge you?
- How does asking the Lord to help you discern affect how you discern?
- How does discernment help you, when you pray for another person?
- How do discernment and obedience go together?

The Knowledge of His Presence

'Then said Jesus unto them, When ye have lifted up the Son of man, then shall ye know that I am he, and that I do nothing of myself; but as my Father hath taught me, I speak these things.'
(John 8:28)

We read in John 8:29:

'And he that sent me is with me: the Father hath not left me alone; for I do always those things that please him.'

How was this possible? Jesus explains further:

'Then said Jesus to those Jews which believed on Him, If ye continue in my word, then are ye my disciples indeed; And ye shall know the truth, and the truth shall make you free. They answered Him, We be Abraham's seed, and were never in bondage to any man: how sayest thou, Ye shall be made free? Jesus answered them, Verily, verily, I say unto you, Whosoever committeth sin is the servant of sin. And the servant abideth not in the house forever: but the Son abideth ever. If the Son therefore shall make you free, ye shall be free indeed.'

(vv. 31–36)

We need to live free from sin and alive to Jesus, pleasing Him in every way. When we live a life pleasing to the Lord, He will never leave us alone, but will be with us in all that He guides us to do. We will value our prayer time and come to a knowledge of His presence and the reality of coming to know the Father in a glorious way. When we come to know the Father, it is He that raises us up to a new realm of walking in Him and it is His desire for us to walk even as Jesus walked. Mark 4:37–41 shows us a wonderful story explaining this:

> *'And there arose a great storm of wind, and the waves beat into the ship, so that it was now full. And he was in the hinder part of the ship, asleep on a pillow: and they awake him, and say unto him, Master, carest thou not that we perish? And he arose, and rebuked the wind, and said unto the sea, Peace, be still. And the wind ceased, and there was a great calm. And he said unto them, Why are ye so fearful? how is it that ye have no faith? And they feared exceedingly, and said one to another, What manner of man is this, that even the wind and the sea obey him?'*

I asked the Lord to explain this story to me. For one thing, how could He be asleep in such a storm? And why did He rebuke His disciples? The Lord answered both my questions. The disciples were living in the earthly realm and Jesus was living in the heavenly realm. Jesus had spent hours in prayer to the Father. He was now *so* at peace, *so* full of the Father's love, power and authority that the storm did not bother Him at all! He was having a nice sleep. But the disciples, fearful of the storm, woke Him up and Jesus was so full of the Father's peace that He merely stood up and rebuked the wind and said to the sea, 'Be still!' and there was a great calm. What was inside Jesus? The power and authority of God within Jesus was far stronger than the storm so the wind and the sea obeyed and Jesus rebuked the disciples for their unbelief. After all, they had seen the healings and the miracles every day, yet

they were still living in the earthly realm, instead of rising up
to live in the heavenly realm in which Jesus walked.

This is explained in 1 John 4:4,

> *'Ye are of God, little children, and have overcome them: because
> greater is he that is in you, than he that is in the world.'*

How many of us are still living in the earthly realm, only
seeing how large the waves are (how large our problems
are, our sicknesses and hurts) instead of rising up with Jesus
above our problems, *above* our sicknesses and *above* our hurts in
prayer?

When we rise up in Christ, He gives us victory in our lives
and we rise up above every problem and take command over
every one of them, just as Jesus took command over the
storm. It is here that we really come to know God and His
power and authority, the same power and authority that He
wants to give to *us*. It is here that He fills us with His Holy
Spirit, giving us the victory. In prayer we learn to live in the
heavenly realm while our feet still walk on this earth. That
is what Jesus did all the time and He wants us to live like
Him too.

It is so exciting to discover the possibilities in Him and it is
amazing when we discover who we really are *in Him*. We are
His sons and daughters of heaven, able to live in the heavenly
realm here on earth and able, not only to claim victory over
our lives in Him, but also do effective exploits for Him. Jesus
wants us to walk in this heavenly realm not only for our own
victory, but also to equip us to take victory to others, so
that they too are delivered, healed and set free to know the
Lord.

For too long the Church has lived far below her potential
and calling, but when the people finally *do* wake up to who
they are in Christ and stand up for what is right, then the devil
gets defeated. Let us not wait any longer, but rise up in Christ

into the glorious victory that He wants to give to each one of us. Let us act upon the promise given in 1 John 3:22:

> *'And whatsoever we ask, we receive of him, because we keep his commandments, and do those things that are pleasing in his sight.'*

In John 8:29 Jesus declares:

> *'And he that sent me is with me: the Father hath not left me alone; for I do always those things that please him.'*

He has not left *us* alone either. He has sent His Holy Spirit to dwell within our hearts and this is the greatest gift and privilege and comfort we can ever know. Colossians 2:6–7 says:

> *'As ye have therefore received Christ Jesus the Lord, so walk ye in him: Rooted and built up in him, and stablished in the faith, as ye have been taught, abounding therein with thanksgiving.'*

Verses 9–10 underline this:

> *'For in him dwelleth all the fulness of the Godhead bodily. And ye are complete in him, which is the head of all principality and power.'*

Simply accept and treasure these promises and act upon them.

What is the depth of this experience? Who of us can share all that we may experience? Yet what the Bible says brings us to a greater and deeper understanding as to the beauty and privilege of abiding fully in Christ, rooted and grounded in His immense love which will cause us to live more and more in Him and less and less in the things of the world, for our hearts will be captured by His great love, causing us to begin to live our lives from within His presence, rather than just from the earthly realm.

In this place in Christ, we are connected to Him with our hearts and, through this connection, we stay constantly in an attitude of prayer. That means living within His presence and from His presence, being able to hear Him and obey Him as we work on earth. In the world we are taught to use our common sense and wisdom in everyday living, making daily decisions that constantly call for our attention, *yet* we must be ready to obey His voice when He speaks. All the serious decisions that I have to make, I make *only* in prayer. I write sermons or books only in prayer. I solve problems in prayer and difficulties I take to the Lord in prayer. I lift up people in prayer. I receive a lot of invitations to various countries so I always lift up these invitations in prayer so that I make the right decisions. I try to do *only* the Father's will. Prayer will help us to understand what the Father's will is for us and to carry it out.

When we begin to live in this place in Christ, His words of wisdom can flow from within us when we speak. His thoughts can become our thoughts and we begin to live out His way through our lives. We begin to become more Christ-like and all our priorities change, enabling us to give ourselves to His work in every way, from walking in obedience to being willing to go to places or give of our substance or money for His work. His priorities have become our priorities so giving to His cause is as important as our own agenda.

I believe there are different levels of knowing God, just as there are different levels of knowing a person. As it takes time to know a person, so it also takes time in prayer to know God and hear His voice.

Jesus knew His Father at the highest levels and therefore moved at the highest levels of obedience and miracle-working power. In the same way, by giving ourselves to much prayer, we too will come to know the Father at a higher level and the higher the level of yielded-ness, the stronger the anointing will become upon our lives.

God is looking for people who will pray and are prepared to surrender their lives to Him in happy, yielded obedience. It does not matter who you are or what job you do. All that matters is that you love God and put Him first in your life.

At the beginning of the ministry which the Lord gave me, He called me to fast and pray constantly for four days. So, for four days I stayed in my room in the glorious presence of God. He taught me so much. When He told me to stop the fast, I cried, as I did not want to leave His beautiful presence. So He assured me that He would come with me wherever I went.

So I ended the fast and went outside to teach a woman who had made an appointment for a private riding lesson. She noticed a change in me and wanted to know what had happened. So I told her about the four-day fast. The lesson ended with her dismounting from her horse, kneeling down against the mounting block to receive Jesus as her Lord and Saviour. This was just the beginning and there appears to be no end to what the Lord teaches us about the knowledge of His presence.

I came back from New Zealand in February 2008, having heard God speak so clearly, yet having only a partial understanding of what He was trying to tell me. He had clearly told me that the devil was trying to steal from me my greatest asset, my time with Him in prayer, and I was to change my priorities but this was not easily done.

After arriving home in England, the work was so much that I ended up just barely keeping up with the emergencies and tasks that had to be done in order to carry on. I ended up working until midnight and sometimes to 1 a.m. and up at 8 a.m. to start again. This went on until the end of May, causing me to become more and more tired and to give less and less time to prayer. No matter what we tried to do, staff just did not come and the three of us were becoming very over-worked. On 1st June, 2008, Wilfrid and I took our first time away together since 1983 when we were first married and headed for eight days in Florida but we were too tired to do anything, even too tired to visit Disneyland. Wilfrid was recovering from two weeks in hospital and even got sick on this holiday and I arrived back with the worst 'flu I have ever had which put me in bed for ten days. Then the Lord spoke: 'If one tries to work cut-off from the relationship and power of God, the works become dead works, devoid of the life and compassion of God's breath upon them.'

These words struck deep within me, so I looked up every scripture relating to work from Genesis to Revelation and received from God something truly wonderful. Here are a few of the scriptures. In Job 1:10 Satan speaks to God about Job,

> '. . . thou hast blessed the work of his hands, and his substance is increased in the land.'

It is interesting to note that Satan hates it if we get it right and will make it his job to intervene. Why? Psalm 141:4 speaks of base works:

> 'Incline not my heart to any evil thing, to practise wicked works with men that work iniquity: and let me not eat of their dainties.'

Proverbs 16:3 says instead:

> 'Commit thy works unto the LORD, and thy thoughts shall be established.'

It is interesting that committing our works to the Lord should establish our thoughts. Proverbs 24:12 goes on to explain it further:

'If thou sayest, Behold, we knew it not; doth not he that pondereth the heart consider it? and he that keepeth thy soul, doth not he know it? and shall not he render to every man according to his works?'

Does this say we have no excuse? We either pray about a work or think about a work before we do it. Or do we just go into it without thought and without a plan? And if we fail to plan, we plan to fail. What quality of work can be achieved without plan or thought?

'I have seen all the works that are done under the sun; and, behold, all is vanity and vexation of spirit.' (Ecclesiastes 1:14)

Our motives are now considered.
Ecclesiastes 12:14 says,

'For God shall bring every work into judgment, with every secret thing, whether it be good, or whether it be evil.'

Jeremiah in his prayer in chapter 32:19 acknowledges that the Lord is,

'Great in counsel, and mighty in work: for thine eyes are open upon all the ways of the sons of men: to give every one according to his ways, and according to the fruit of his doings.'

1 Corinthians 3:13 says,

'Every man's work shall be made manifest: for the day shall declare it, because it shall be revealed by fire; and the fire shall try every man's work of what sort it is.'

We see from these scriptures that our works are important to the Lord. So how do we do them the Lord's way? Ephesians 2:10 says:

> *'For we are his workmanship, created in Christ Jesus unto good*
> *works, which God hath before ordained that we should walk in*
> *them.'*

If it has been 'ordained' that we walk in good works from
the foundation of the world, our works must become of the
utmost importance.

> *'Therefore leaving the principles of the doctrine of Christ, let us go on*
> *unto perfection; not laying again the foundation of repentance from*
> *dead works . . .'*   (Hebrews 6:1)

Then Hebrews 9:14 says:

> *'How much more shall the blood of Christ, who through the eternal*
> *Spirit offered himself without spot to God, purge your conscience*
> *from dead works to serve the living God?'*

This is speaking about more than turning from evil works, it is
also talking about turning from dead works devoid of the
blessing of God, works that are not done unto the Lord in
service. By this time, I was really receiving the message, that
although I had prepared all that I was to do for the Lord in
prayer and He had blessed it, the more mundane things that
had to be done daily, I had done in my strength alone, thus
turning them into dead works. So I asked, 'Lord, are You sure
that I must commit *every* work that I do to You?' The Lord
replied, 'Yes, every work.'

I realised that while I had been sick in bed, the Lord had
released our staff. We now had a full-time cleaner, a Christian
from Asia, plus a secretary to relieve me of much of the work.
All of a sudden, I could relax into a more normal lifestyle. I
had time to prepare in prayer properly and I restarted the staff
prayer time every morning. Unity resulted. There was enough
time to give to the people who came and they left healed,

delivered and closer to God and Wilfrid also received a healing miracle. Everything started to work well with a new joy among us. A breakthrough had been made. The Lord then showed me Ecclesiastes 9:7 which reads:

> *'Go thy way, eat thy bread with joy, and drink thy wine with a merry heart; for God now accepteth thy works.'*

(I don't drink wine but I understood.) And also Proverbs 31:31,

> *'Give her of the fruit of her hands; and let her own works praise her in the gates.'*

Then I read three more promises:

> *'I know thy works: behold, I have set before thee an open door, and no man can shut it: for thou hast a little strength, and hast kept my word, and hast not denied my name.'*   (Revelation 3:8)

> *'And he that overcometh, and keepeth my works unto the end, to him will I give power over the nations . . .'*   (Revelation 2:26)

> *'And I heard a voice from heaven saying unto me, Write, Blessed are the dead which die in the Lord from henceforth: Yea, saith the Spirit, that they may rest from their labours; and their works do follow them.'*   (Revelation 14:13)

This is how Jesus lived. He spent much time in the Father's presence. He brought everything into His presence and received detailed revelation and instruction for every work He did and the result was outstanding. The works of Jesus were perfect and nobody could fault Him. The most glorious fact is that we too can walk this way in Him. As we learn from God, in His presence, and receive precise instructions, and as we receive from Him His strength, His vitality, His peace and His blessing and we go forth to serve Him in the task, we will no longer limit Him, we will no longer miss His divine appointments and our dull or dead works will come alive and be blessed and victorious in Him.

There is no better way to live and work than this. Not only that, but His presence will be with us continually.

It is also not how much we can do for the Lord that matters, but who we are in Christ, our heart connection of love in Christ – until we can say 'All who I am, all that I have, all that I ever hope to be, is yours, Lord, forever.'

Some questions to think about:

- What does John 8:28 mean to you?
- Why should we only do what pleases the Father?
- What was inside Jesus that was more powerful than the storm? Explain.
- Why did Jesus rebuke His disciples, and what happens when we rise up into the presence of God?
- The devil will go to all lengths to take away our greatest asset, our time with God in prayer. Why?

Seeing from within the Heavenly Realm

'I speak that which I have seen with My Father.'
(John 8:38)

John 8:38–39 continues:

> '... and ye do that which ye have seen from your father. They answered and said unto him, Abraham is our father. Jesus saith unto them, If ye were Abraham's children, ye would do the works of Abraham.'

Who is our father?

> 'Jesus said unto them, If God were your Father, ye would love me: for I proceeded forth and came from God; neither came I of myself, but he sent me.'   (John 8:42)

Whoever is of God hears the words of God. In John 8:47 Jesus says,

> 'He that is of God heareth God's words: ye therefore hear them not, because ye are not of God.'

Who tells us what to do? Is it God or man? Are we hearing the words of God? Are we doing what we see with our Father? In John 9:4 Jesus says,

> *'I must work the works of him that sent me, while it is day: the night cometh, when no man can work.'*

Jesus is still with us through His Holy Spirit, but night is coming on the whole earth. We need to do His works now, while we still can.

Jesus also saw the Father do some unusual things. John 9:6–7 says,

> *'When he had thus spoken, he spat on the ground, and made clay of the spittle, and he anointed the eyes of the blind man with the clay, and said unto him, Go, wash in the pool of Siloam, (which is by interpretation, Sent). He went his way therefore, and washed, and came seeing.'*

Sometimes we too will see the Father show us some unusual things and we need to be obedient to what we see Him doing, so that the miracle will happen. I believe the Lord does this to keep us on our toes, to keep us relying on Him.

In October 2007 I spoke on the radio and as a result a woman phoned me from Leeds in Yorkshire about an issue of blood from which she had suffered for over six months and she asked me to pray for her healing. I prayed but felt I had not heard God, so I said to her, 'If you are not healed by tomorrow, please phone me.' She did indeed phone me, still not healed. I asked the Lord what to do and He said, 'Tell her to lift her arm and touch the hem of my garment in the heavenly spiritual realm.' So, I told her to do so. She was walking down the road at the time, talking on her mobile phone but she obeyed and reached up her arm and touched the hem of His garment in the spirit realm. She was instantly healed. She waited a week to test her healing and then caught the train to Oxford to testify of her healing at our Monday night prayer group.

In John 9:31 a blind man who was healed said,

> *'Now we know that God heareth not sinners: but if any man be a worshipper of God, and doeth his will, him he heareth.'*

It is through hearing God in worship that we can obey Him and do His will on earth. But how do we hear God? The answer comes in John 10:3–4 where Jesus speaks about the shepherd of the sheep,

> *'To him the porter openeth; and the sheep hear his voice: and he calleth his own sheep by name, and leadeth them out. And when he putteth forth his own sheep, he goeth before them, and the sheep follow him: for they know his voice.'*

In John 10:14–16 Jesus explains this further:

> *'I am the good shepherd, and know my sheep, and am known of mine. As the Father knoweth me, even so know I the Father: and I lay down my life for the sheep. And other sheep I have, which are not of this fold: them also I must bring, and they shall hear my voice; and there shall be one fold, and one shepherd.'*

I would like to make a few observations about this:

1. We come to know and hear God by spending time with Him in prayer and worship.
2. When we hear Him, He goes before us to lead us.
3. We who know the Father's voice will not waver but will follow Him in confidence, for we are able to hear Him clearly step by step.

4. As we follow Him ever more closely in prayer and in listening to Him speak, He will show us more and more until we are able to see with the Father and speak of those things we have seen with the Father.

As Jesus grew in His glorious relationship with the Father, so His miracles and healings grew in size accordingly. In John 11:40–44 Jesus said,

> *'Said I not unto thee, that, if thou wouldest believe, thou shouldest see the glory of God? Then they took away the stone from the place where the dead was laid. And Jesus lifted up his eyes, and said, Father, I thank thee that thou hast heard me. And I knew that thou hearest me always: but because of the people which stand by I said it, that they may believe that thou hast sent me. And when he thus had spoken, he cried with a loud voice, Lazarus, come forth. And he that was dead came forth . . .*

The more we come to know our Father in heaven, the more we will hear Him, the more we will be able to see what He is doing, in heaven and on earth, and when we are able to see what He is doing, the greater will be our faith. The greater our faith, the greater the miracles and healings that will take place.

On one of the visits to Kenya we visited a woman with such bad arthritis that both knee joints had fused solid and she could not move them at all so that she could neither stand on them nor place them on the ground from the chair on which she was sitting. They had been fused for over one year.

I saw in the spirit realm that Jesus was going to heal her so I said to her, 'Within two minutes you will be able to walk.' I then prayed for her and told her to move her knees up and down and movement began to come into her knees. I then said, 'In the name of Jesus, get up and walk.' And she raised herself up and began to walk. 'As you walk further, more healing will come.' And she began to walk more and more freely. Within minutes she could walk up and down steps and cried 'Thank You, Jesus, thank You, Jesus.' The next day she ran to greet me, so overjoyed with her healing.

In John 12:25–26, Jesus said,

> 'He that loveth his life shall lose it; and he that hateth his life in this world shall keep it unto life eternal. If any man serve me, let him follow me; and where I am, there shall also my servant be: if any man serve me, him will my Father honour.'

In John 12:44–45, Jesus cried and said,

> 'He that believeth on me, believeth not on me, but on him that sent me. And he that seeth me seeth him that sent me.'

These are wonderful words with deep significance, for in serving God we sometimes have to go into dangerous places. We have to go regardless of what we may have to face. I heard from an evangelist who realised he may even be facing death, 'Who is afraid of heaven? To leave this world doing the Father's will is to leave it with honour and enter into eternal life with Jesus.'

When we see Jesus, we see the Father also. Jesus raised people from the dead and then He Himself rose from the dead on the third day in complete victory over every evil force. When we believe Jesus, we are placing our trust in our living God who is also able to save us from every evil force and give us eternal life. Who better can we believe and trust? No-one.

Earlier in John 5:19, we read of Jesus seeing what the Father is doing and obeying Him and here in John 8:38 we read that Jesus spoke about seeing with His Father. This is even closer relationship. What is this actually saying? Can spending time in prayer actually enable us to see with the Father? Is seeing with the Father seeing with our physical eyes or with the eyes of our understanding or in the area of visions and prophecy?

The relationship the Father has with each one of us is unique and He will speak to us through different ways according to our character.

My daughter Rebecca is a prophetic artist. She will ask the Lord how to paint each picture and the Lord will show her. He even showed her visions of heaven when she was sixteen years old and she described these in great detail, exactly as they are told in the book of Revelation. Rebecca had not read this part of the Bible and she realised that the only reason for her being a good artist is that the Lord has given her the gift and ability and this has drawn her closer to Him.

The Lord is the source of all life. We are sparks of life created in the image of God. When we draw near to God, He gives us life in more abundance. He gives us more understanding, more revelation, more of His life, strength and supernatural power. We grow in our relationship with the Father and we also grow in our faith and this powerfully affects our life and ministry.

Seeing with our Father is a glorious privilege, as He shows us what He is doing on earth and the role He wants each one of us to have. People who move in prophetic gifting will be able to see and understand what they see in this realm and the Father will also show them things before they happen. This will help equip and prepare the Church for what is to come. Old Testament prophets spent most of their lives in prayer in order to hear and see what the Lord was doing with accuracy, so that they could guide kings and lead the people back to God. Moving in this realm in our day requires a similar amount of time in prayer if we are to be true prophets and workers for God.

Seeing with God leads us on to power with God. In Habakkuk 3:4, we read,

> *'And his brightness was as the light; he had horns coming out of his hand: and there was the hiding of his power.'*

This speaks of the brightness of God and the hiding of His power in His hand. In Matthew 28:18–20 we read,

> '*And Jesus came and spake unto them, saying, All power is given unto me in heaven and in earth. Go ye therefore, and teach all nations, baptizing them in the name of the Father, and of the Son, and of the Holy Ghost: Teaching them to observe all things whatsoever I have commanded you: and, lo, I am with you alway, even unto the end of the world. Amen.*'

Here we read that all power is given to Jesus and when we do what He has commanded us, **He is with us always**.

In Ephesians 3:7, Paul says,

> '*Whereof I was made a minister, according to the gift of the grace of God given unto me by the effectual working of his power.*'

In Philippians 3:9–10 Paul joyfully expressed his wish,

> '[to] *be found **in him**, not having mine own righteousness, which is of the law, but that which is through the faith of Christ, the righteousness which is of God by faith: That I may know him, and the power of his resurrection, and the fellowship of his sufferings, being made conformable unto his death.*'   (emphasis added)

It is through living in Him and walking in Him that you will come to that place where you will see with Him and receive power with Him, as you yield to Him in such a way that He is able to do His work with you and through you, enabling power to be released with Him as He is doing His work on earth with you, that is, at one through the Holy Spirit and in action with Him. Experiencing power with God simply means He is doing it with you. This is a dimension of living not often seen today but a few are living in it.

In September 2008, I had the opportunity to go to Estonia

with David Hathaway's Eurovision and David put me in charge of the healing team. On the Friday of that week thousands of people came forward to receive Jesus in one of the largest stadiums in Europe and then David prayed for the sick and many were healed in their seats. He then called for those who needed prayer to come forward and called me to pray for them. They filled up the front and I went down the lines praying for them and watched as Jesus healed them. But I was praying too slowly, so David tapped me on the shoulder and said, 'There are too many for you to pray for them like this. There is only time for a few seconds for each one.' This I found difficult, as I did not want to leave anybody half-healed with insufficient faith to receive their complete healing.

The next day there was more time and I spent about four hours praying for two rooms plus the passage, full of sick people, and many, many more received their healing.

On the third morning of the conference, I was to speak on television about some of the healings I had seen and, as I shared them, a horrible doubt entered my mind, 'What if one of those people is not fully healed?'

That night one of those healed ran to the front, with thousands of others, to receive Jesus as Lord and I nearly cried over her beautiful faith and also my own doubt of that morning. So I repented and literally cast every doubt, no matter how small, out of my being.

David prayed for the sick again and called those who needed prayer to come forward. The front filled up again. He called me forward to pray for them. As I went forward, the Holy Spirit was so powerful that, as I laid hands on people, they were healed in seconds: ears popped open, eyes were healed and pain left in a second. This was a new level of faith and anointing I never imagined was possible, as I experienced not power 'from' God but power 'with' God, as He healed these people instantly through a simple touch.

A week later I went to hear David Hathaway again, this time speaking at Hollybush in West Yorkshire, England on 'How to receive power with God'. This brought the Scriptures alive to me, as this new dimension or level of walking in Christ began to become more real in my life as he showed us how to struggle in prayer to achieve it, so that more people respond to Christ.

I have travelled a lot and have seen other evangelists in action, but rarely have I seen results like those I saw with David Hathaway. I have seen the wind of the Holy Spirit enter the stadium in the 1980 Renewal Conference in South Africa while Reinhard Bonnke was ministering and I experienced it once in Kenya in the 'Fire over Kenya' conference in 2001 while I was ministering, but never have I seen real genuine healings manifest in a second, at a simple touch, as in David's crusade.

One has to live in Christ before one can see with Him. One has to see *with* Him before one can receive power with Him and this can only be done through prayer. I mean deep, yielded, effectual prayer and communication with the Lord Himself, praying through to victory. This is often travailing prayer, 'hard work' prayer, fighting against the forces of darkness until one prays right through into the very light and presence of God, where true victory is found.

There was still more though that I needed to learn with this struggle in prayer. David Hathaway was speaking on television about this choice facing him in prison behind the Iron Curtain. The easy way was to stay alive in prison for ten years, waiting to be released eventually; the hard way, however, was by struggling in prayer to be released on the very day David had agreed with God. I looked up this part in David's book *Czechmate* where he was thrown in prison for smuggling Bibles into Russia. I read about his dialogue with God in prayer and of his struggle to keep up believing faith in what the Scriptures said, against the backdrop of being imprisoned with no realistic chance of being released in the natural order to things. At one point he got sick and then repented of lack of faith and prayed until the presence of God restored his faith. David was then released on the exact day agreed with God, his birthday, by Harold Wilson. This great lesson in faith then opened up to the very successful and powerful Eurovision mission into Russia and Europe through David, causing revival to break out wherever he goes.

The Lord revealed to me that our main battle is in our minds where both positive and negative thoughts constantly influence our thinking. We have to learn to get victory over the negatives in our minds if we are to have faith for a certain thing. We need to be able to rise up above the temporal realm in prayer for this to truly happen. Knowing God alone can conquer the negative thoughts of our minds, as His presence enters in with His victory, His love, His power, His enabling. It is then that we begin to see 'with' Him and attain power with Him to walk a new dynamic faith of victory. It is in the heavenly realm of God's glorious and holy presence that one can find power with Him to go to where He sends you in His strength and His victory, to do the work He has given us to do on earth. When we see how unimaginably great our God is, we can have faith and power with Him to overcome every negative force the devil will throw our way.

Jeremiah 33:2–3 says,

> *'Thus saith the* LORD *the maker thereof, the* LORD *that formed it, to establish it; the* LORD *is his name; Call unto me, and I will answer thee, and shew thee great and mighty things, which thou knowest not.'*

Yes, let us call unto Him, let us communicate with Him, allow Him to show us great and mighty things, to see with Him who we are in Him, and to receive power with Him to bring victory in our lives and to the lives of others on this earth.

Some questions to think about:

- Why is it important to see with the Father?
- What do we learn from John 11:40–44?
- What does seeing with God lead to?
- How do we get victory over the negatives in our mind?

Prayer House, Standlake Ranch: Erumere Esther reaches up to take hold of the hem of Jesus' garment in the spirit realm and is instantly healed of an issue of blood for six months. She was walking in town talking to Suzanne on her mobile phone at the time. This photo was taken a week later when she came by train to testify of her healing at a Standlake prayer meeting.

CHAPTER

9

The Authority of Jesus' Name

*'For I have not spoken of myself; but the Father which sent
me, he gave me a commandment, what I should say, and
what I should speak. And I know that his commandment is
life everlasting: whatsoever I speak therefore, even as the
Father said unto me, so I speak.'*
(John 12:49–50)

In John 13 Jesus prepared His disciples for the greatest event
the world had ever known, the greatest gift the world could
ever receive, the greatest encounter for every life that receives
Him: His death and resurrection from the dead, leading to our
salvation and everlasting life. Jesus spoke not on His own
authority but on His Father's who sent Him. He could speak
from His authority for Jesus knew the Father and knew why
He was on this earth. He knew the Father so well that He
could trust Him fully to do what He said that He would do.
Jesus knew that He would rise from the dead. Jesus also knew
that God loved the world so much that, through sending Him,
He would give eternal life to every person who received
Him for He says in John 13:20,

*'Verily, verily, I say unto you, He that receiveth whomsoever I send
receiveth me; and he that receiveth me receiveth him that sent me.'*

This is speaking about us. God sent Jesus. Now Jesus sends us and we too must speak only what He tells us to speak. When we speak or pray for others in the Name of Jesus, He gives us the authority of His Name. In the authority of the Name of Jesus, we can cast out demons, sickness and pain. The more we do this, the more able we will become in using His authority.

I asked the Lord one day, 'How is it that some evangelists have more anointing and authority than others?' The Lord replied with the words of John the Baptist in John 3:34,

> 'For he whom God hath sent speaketh the words of God: for God giveth not the Spirit by measure unto him.'

Now, this is speaking about Jesus but, as God sent Jesus, so Jesus sends us and He too does not give the Spirit by measure. He gives us the Holy Spirit fully. It depends on us. How much anointing we receive in prayer, and the level of authority in which we walk, will depend on how much authority we believe we have received in the Name of Jesus over sickness and demons. The problem with us is that we tend to look at the size of the sickness or the demon, rather than to the mighty power of the Name of Jesus. I have to confess that I struggle with this. Praying for one man, paralysed from the chest down and in a wheelchair for several years, was already a challenge but when I was told that eight inches of his spine had been removed, I am afraid I lost faith for that miracle and did not have the faith to pray for him. Afterwards, I confessed my lack of faith to the Lord and I felt that it was my fault that he was still in a wheelchair. Yes, these things are a struggle for us and each of us must work it out with the Lord, as we face greater challenges in the people for whom we pray.

Jesus believed that He had full and complete authority from His Father and exercised it to perfection. If Jesus had prayed for that man in the wheelchair, he would have been healed, for spare parts are no problem in heaven. I believe our battle is more in the spiritual realm than in the physical realm, for the spiritual realm is stronger than the physical realm.

When Jesus rebuked the storm and said to the waves, 'Peace, be still', was He actually speaking to the wind and the sea or was He talking to the spiritual realm that caused the storm? Jesus always went to the root cause. Well, surely, it is the invisible spirit realm that can blow up a storm? So, to speak to it will certainly work and be effective. Whatever it was that Jesus rebuked, the authority within Him was infinitely greater than the storm and we have this assurance in 1 John 4:4,

> *'Ye are of God, little children, and have overcome them: because greater is he that is in you, than he that is in the world.'*

If only we fully believed these words, we would rise up and take all the authority that we have been given in the Name of Jesus. Think of what we could do in the Name of Jesus. Just as every knee must bow and every tongue confess that Jesus is Lord, all must obey the Name of Jesus. This gives us the authority of Jesus over every sickness which has a name and every demon which has a name. As we believe we have this authority, we will take hold of the authority of Jesus' Name and exercise it over every sickness and every demon, until we see every sickness and every demon bow the knee and leave at the mention of the Name of Jesus.

In John 14:3–4 Jesus gives us one of His greatest promises,

> *'And if I go and prepare a place for you, I will come again, and receive you unto myself; that where I am, there ye may be also. And whither I go ye know, and the way ye know.'*

Jesus had full confidence in God to face the cross, through His great love for us, knowing that the Father would raise Him from the dead. As we obey Jesus with full confidence, and know His promises, we also will be able to face every challenge, every healing and every deliverance, believing and knowing that, as we speak in the authority of the powerful Name of Jesus, Jesus will confirm His word. This is the faith in Him that He is calling each one of us to live by, including me.

James 5:16 says,

> '*Confess your faults one to another, and pray one for another, that ye may be healed. The effectual fervent prayer of a righteous man availeth much.*'

This tells us that righteousness and authority go together. Jesus was the most righteous man who ever lived and He knew His authority over evil. Therefore He had full confidence in God to raise Him from the dead. God did just that on the third day.

As sin leads to worse sin, and the flesh gets weaker under the power of sin, so too when we turn from sin, and yield ourselves to righteousness, we become stronger and stronger in righteousness which leads to holiness. It is then that our prayers will be heard by God and will bring about a change. This will also clear the channel of our hearts and lives for the Lord to pour His power and authority through in victory over every sickness or demonic power. Through this, God gives us the authority of the Name of Jesus to cast out demons and sickness and pain, all of which will obey, for Jesus is far stronger and every knee must bow and every tongue confess that Jesus Christ is Lord. As for me, I will pursue righteousness every day of my life, remembering that repentant believers are already clothed in the righteousness of Christ, as 2 Corinthians 5:21 promises,

> '*For he hath made him to be sin for us, who knew no sin; that we might be made the righteousness of God in him.*'

On October 4th, 2008, I was on the way to London to speak to a meeting of 'Women Aglow'. I got on the bus at 6 a.m. and, seeing it already full of people, climbed up to the top deck and sat in the front row. It was still dark.

Slowly the horizon turned to gold in the distance and the sun began to rise, shining golden beams through the sky, causing light to burst forth, piercing the darkness, to herald a new day. Here eternity and the temporary realm meet in extraordinary unity, sparking the promise of another day of light in exhilarating victory over darkness. Yes, the darkness of sin may have crept into our world but light can overcome it in minutes, when truth is revealed and a person turns from darkness to light, from evil to righteousness and from death to everlasting life.

The sun rises into the skies and shines with full authority and full light across the lands, bringing life and warmth and beauty to all she touches. The birds fly up and young calves prance in the fields, while humans, almost without noticing all of this, drive the motorways of the temporary.

There is an authority that the world *cannot* touch, the authority of the Word that created all of Heaven and earth; the authority that separated light from darkness and created day, the authority that came to earth to bring a new day to the souls of mankind, to deliver us from eternal darkness and sin and bring us all into *all* truth and righteousness through receiving Jesus as Lord and Saviour. That authority we come to know as we connect with our eternal God who is timeless and powerful and who spans past, present and future and Who holds the power of the universe in the palms of His hands.

He who raised Jesus from the dead even gives us, who have received Christ, the authority of the powerful Name of Jesus to cast out all manner of sicknesses and demons and the authority to bring the light of Christ to millions of people on this earth.

This power, authority and victory in Christ is freely available to us. We must rise up in Him; the skies are no limit. In prayer we can soar into the presence of God and bring His riches down to mankind, riches upon riches that no money can buy – health and peace, joy and love, light and eternal life.

As we wait upon Him in worship and prayer, heaven invades our very souls and spirits, filling them with *His* light, power, strength and authority. As His words, spoken through our mouths, rise like the sun over people's lives, they inspire enduring changes and bring into eternal life. Eternity will *overcome* the temporary, in the glorious light of God's presence forever.

I put my pen and notebook away as the bus arrived at Victoria Station and I caught the Underground to the venue. After an excellent Women Aglow breakfast, we sang some choruses and then I was called forward to speak. I began the message with what the Lord had revealed to me on the bus and the people responded fully. I then prayed for the sick and watched the Lord heal every one of them. Others then testified of their healings received and kept since last year.

When we grasp just what authority we have in Christ, we can command sickness and demons to come out. When sickness or demonic powers realize who you are in Christ and see that you *mean* it, they have to leave, for every knee must bow and every name confess that Jesus Christ is Lord. When we really get a revelation of how *great* our God is and who we are in Him, nothing will be able to stop us.

When I returned home, an email arrived from India to say that our 3,343 evangelists had already planted 10,822 churches and with three months still to go. Yes, we have the authority of Christ to change villages and cities and even nations in Jesus' Name.

Verse 50 of John 12 goes onto say, *'And I know that his*

commandment is life everlasting: whatsoever I speak therefore, even as the Father said unto me, so I speak.'

Going to India in November 2008 brought this verse to a new understanding. That also linked with the power and authority we have just spoken of.

On the way to a church the Lord spoke to me to speak on the stretching out the paralysed hand. I then went on to share how I prayed for a man who had a crippled hand for twenty years. I said, 'In the name of Jesus stretch out your hand.' He argued, 'You know I cannot do that; I haven't been able to do that for twenty years.' 'Do you want to get healed?' I asked. 'Of course I want to get healed.' 'Then get your brain out of the way. In the name of Jesus stretch out your hand,' I ordered, and the man stretched out his hand. Jesus completely healed the man's hand, to his utmost amazement and joy.

'It is who you believe,' I went on, 'the world or the word. The world is spiritually dead, cut off from God due to the fall of man. They are therefore restricted to the natural realm only. But those who receive Jesus as Lord are reborn spiritually to eternal life. They are no longer bound to the natural realm only, but can rise up in Christ into the supernatural realm where miracles become normal.

'Now if you believe these verses I have just read, put your own hand on your sickness or pain and receive your healing now in Jesus' name and when you are healed put your hand up high in the air.'

The hands began to go up, so I invited a couple to come and testify to what Jesus had done for them. The first to testify was a lady deaf in one ear but now, after the prayer, she could hear with both ears. The second was a man who almost shouted out into the megaphone, 'I have had a crippled hand for many years but look, see, I can now open my hand, and lift my arm, because Jesus has just healed me now. I am so happy.' 'This sermon was just for you,' I told him, and he went to sit down.

We must realise we are bringing eternal life in Jesus to this world, but why are we not all going? Why are we so restricted in sharing this glorious news of Jesus?

I know for myself how I was restricted until evangelist David Hathaway said, 'Go', and yet it is in the Bible all the time. First it is because we believe the devil that we cannot do it. Or people say we are too young, too old, too weak, or only a girl – as I did. Or do we just lack the love for the lost or receive the negative attitude of the world towards the evangelists? Or do we need a drop of the Father's love on our lives to pop to top, so to say? If so, we can receive this through prayer.

For me David's 'Go' was like the starting gates opening in a horse race and I was off at full gallop into the greatest victory race the world has ever known and I cannot slow down.

The energy that has been released within me to do this work is almost explosive and nothing can stop me. God's purpose has filled my heart, energised my feet, and flows from my mouth with such conviction that even Hindu priests are coming to Christ. Doing only the Father's will has not only become the most important in my life, but has totally enabled me to do what I could never do in my own strength. Sometimes I feel that I am literally being carried and enabled by the Lord Himself and the joy that radiates from this is quite contagious.

Being in the centre of God's will is the most glorious place to be, as well as the safest and the best in every way. Whether one speaks to 1 or 160,000 it does not matter as long as we are in God's will. As the shepherd will leave the 100 sheep to seek out the one lost sheep, so God will do the same and for that purpose He will use you or me. The question is, Will we respond?

> *'And the world passeth away, and the lust thereof: but he that doeth the will of God abideth forever.'* (1 John 2:17)

Our God is a great God, a God of love and compassion. He did not just say He loved us, He put it into action. He sent His only Son Jesus to demonstrate His love, to take our sins upon Himself on the cross that we might be forgiven and be set free.

We too must not just say we love God, we also need to put it into action by telling others this glorious news.

The Lord has also given us His Word and this too we need to put into action in our lives if we are to have full impact on this world of ours. The Word is full of power and authority and trains us in all righteousness. As we study the Word, especially the miracles and healings Jesus did, then step out in faith in them, and the Lord Himself will action them into reality through our lives.

When we yield ourselves to the Lord, He literally clothes us with His presence. It's as if He has His hands around us to guide us and protect us, to encourage and enable us, to then do what we cannot do, heal the sick, create miracles and show Himself as Lord.

Some questions to think about:

- We tend to look at the size of the sickness or demon rather than the mighty power and authority and name of Jesus. How do we overcome this?
- How does righteousness affect authority?
- How do we receive this authority?
- How will the authority of the name of Jesus affect your work for Him?

Suzanne teaching in the Prayer House of her Standlake home.

African with crippled hand and leg after a stroke 20 years ago. I told him to get his brain out of the way and in the name of Jesus to stretch out his hand. Amazed that Jesus instantly healed his crippled hand and arm he raises up his stick to walk on his crippled leg which is now also healed.

Believing Faith

'Believest thou not that I am in the Father, and the Father in me? The words that I speak unto you I speak not of myself: but the Father that dwelleth in me, he doeth the works. Believe me that I am in the Father, and the Father in me: or else believe me for the very works' sake.'

(John 14:10–11)

John 14:12–14 continues,

'Verily, verily, I say unto you, He that believeth on me, the works that I do shall he do also; and greater works than these shall he do; because I go unto my Father. And whatsoever ye shall ask in my name, that will I do, that the Father may be glorified in the Son. If ye shall ask any thing in my name, I will do it.'

What more amazing promise can we have than that? Oh, I feel the presence of the Lord so strongly as I write this. He is calling us to greater faith: 'Yes, My child, I am calling you to be pioneers, I am calling you to be My forerunners. Even as John the Baptist was My forerunner before I physically came on earth, so I call My forerunners now, to prepare My world for the greatest event it has ever seen, My second coming. I am calling forth My forerunners now. I call you to walk in greater faith than that of your fathers. I call you to rise up into a dimension of faith that the world has been waiting for. Believe Me, My children, that I am coming soon. Believe Me, My children, that I have given you authority to tread all over the power of the enemy and he will by no means be able to harm you. Rise up, My children, to this dimension of faith that I am calling you to walk in.'

Thank You, Lord, for this word. Help me, Lord, to walk in You. Help these readers to walk in You too. Please bless the people who are reading this book with Your presence, that they too may rise up and walk in You, in the way You wish us to. Thank You, Jesus.

> *'If ye love me, keep my commandments. And I will pray the Father, and he shall give you another Comforter, that he may abide with you forever; Even the Spirit of truth; whom the world cannot receive, because it seeth him not, neither knoweth him: but ye know him; for he dwelleth with you, and shall be in you. I will not leave you comfortless: I will come to you. Yet a little while, and the world seeth me no more; but ye see me: because I live, ye shall live also.'*
>
> (John 14:15–19)

This promise enables us to believe Jesus in the same way that He believed His Father in heaven, enabling Him to lay down His life for us and die on the cross, taking away our sin and shame. Then He rose on the third day in complete victory over every sin, sickness and demonic thing and ascended to the right hand of the Father, where He is now.

If we believe Jesus, in the same way we too will rise up in the same victory. We will come to know God so well in our prayer time and practical walk that we will no longer limit Him by our unbelief or lack of faith but we will rise up in Him and walk in Him as we should – as His children who know how to walk in victory, who know who we are in Christ, who know the mighty power of the Name of Jesus. In that day, demons will know who we are in Christ and will flee at the very mention of Jesus' Name.

In the rain forest of Ghana, I had to make a courtesy visit to the local king. We entered his courts, shook hands with the king and his twelve elders and sat down before him.

The king stood up and I too stood up and curtsied. He then looked at me and said, 'Greetings. You have a word from God for me.' I had not prepared for this and grabbed my Bible and opened it just anywhere and felt the Lord say, 'Read it.'

> *'See, I have set before thee this day life and good, and death and evil.'*   (Deuteronomy 30:15)

I gulped, thinking, Lord, 'Now what?' 'Give the gospel message.' I gave the gospel message and then returned to Deuteronomy 30:8–9:

> *And thou shalt return and obey the voice of the LORD, and do all his commandments which I command thee this day. And the LORD thy God will make thee plenteous in every work of thine hand, in the fruit of thy body, and in the fruit of thy cattle, and in the fruit of thy land, for good: for the LORD will again rejoice over thee for good, as he rejoiced over thy fathers.'*

I stopped and quickly sat down. The king then said, 'I receive this message from God and I will do it,' and immediately called for his gong gong beater, while I gave a sigh of relief, thanking the Lord for doing it yet again.

The gong gong beater arrived, an elderly thin man with a brass plate and a gong. 'Go into every kraal of the area and command every man, woman and child to come to the 11.00 am crusade in the coconut tree field tomorrow.' The gong gong beater then went on his way to proclaim the message.

The next day about 2,000 people crowded the field; many hundreds of people came to salvation. Many others were healed including five of the king's elders. The king also sent us crates of cool drinks as a gift for the occasion.

Six months later I got an e-mail from the king. He has built churches for the people of his kingdom, and would I send him a few sheets of roofing as a gesture to his people? I gladly responded to his request.

Another time in Pakistan a Muslim happened to be walking on the road in front of the church where I was preaching. When he overheard me mention the Name of Jesus, the asthma he had suffered from for three years left him and he was totally healed. He came into the church shouting, 'Who is this Jesus? I want to know this Jesus! This Jesus has just healed my chest.' All we have to do is speak the Name of Jesus and He will do the work and often He does far more than we can ever think or imagine. As previously mentioned in chapter 5 of this book, people who had demons were unable to enter the prayer tunnel until the demons had left them. Jesus promised in John 14:20,

> 'At that day ye shall know that I am in my Father, and ye in me, and I in you.'

Jesus had the Father living in Him and we have the Holy Spirit living in us and we live in Him. How much more amazing can God's promise be? We can live as close to Jesus as we want to. The more we get to know Him in prayer, the closer we will live in Him and He in us and the more Christ-like we will become, for spending time with Him rubs off on us. In John 14:21, Jesus promises,

> 'He that hath my commandments, and keepeth them, he it is that loveth me: and he that loveth me shall be loved of my Father, and I will love him, and will manifest myself to him.'

How wonderful it is when Jesus manifests Himself to us and makes Himself known to us! Some of us have seen visions of Him. Others have recognized His presence or actions in their midst. Others have heard Him speak clearly. Many of us are able to share times when Jesus has manifested Himself to us in some way and most of us have experienced His love towards us.

As we rise up into the dimension of faith to which the Lord is calling us, to be His witnesses to the lost whom the Lord wants to save, we will experience Christ in our lives so much more. But are we living in this realm? How do we actually connect with heaven? The Lord showed me the following which may help explain.

Jesus connected Himself with heaven through His relationship with His Father in prayer. He lived *from* the heavenly realm while He lived *in* the earthly realm and He has made it possible for us to do the same.

> *'Wherefore, holy brethren, partakers of the heavenly calling, consider the Apostle and High Priest of our profession, Christ Jesus.'*
> (Hebrews 3:1)

Here, the author of Hebrews speaks of us as holy brethren, partakers of the heavenly calling. We have been called to be partakers of the heavenly realm. Paul explains this beautifully in 1 Corinthians 15:45–50:

> *'And so it is written, The first man Adam was made a living soul; the last Adam was made a quickening spirit. Howbeit that was not first which is spiritual, but that which is natural; and afterward that which is spiritual. The first man is of the earth, earthy: the second man is the Lord from heaven. As is the earthy, such are they also that are earthy: and as is the heavenly, such are they also that are heavenly. And as we have borne the image of the earthy, we shall also bear the image of the heavenly. Now this I say, brethren, that*

flesh and blood cannot inherit the kingdom of God; neither doth corruption inherit incorruption.'

Through Jesus' death on the cross, we become reborn to eternal life. We gain access into the heavenly realm through prayer while on earth and our spirits are translated there at physical death. Very few people have been physically raised to heaven. Paul takes this topic even further in his letter to the Ephesians 3:8–12,

> *'Unto me, who am less than the least of all saints, is this grace given, that I should preach among the Gentiles the unsearchable riches of Christ; And to make all men see what is the fellowship of the mystery, which from the beginning of the world hath been hid in God, who created all things by Jesus Christ: To the intent that now unto the principalities and powers in heavenly places might be known by the church the manifold wisdom of God, According to the eternal purpose which he purposed in Christ Jesus our Lord: In whom we have **boldness and access with confidence** by the faith of him.'* (emphasis added)

This is so exciting. In the spiritual realm, we have access into heaven through prayer! This is not just boldness to approach God in prayer, but access through into the very presence of God.

This is the best place to be and, although we may sometimes struggle in prayer to come into this glorious place in the Lord, it is worth it. Our enemy, the devil, will go to all lengths to prevent us reaching this place; he will try to make us very busy or distract us in every possible way. But, when we put prayer first and pursue the Lord face on, as into the wind, with determination and full concentration, we will enter through.

Jesus spent much time in this place and lived from within God's presence. He lived on earth from within the heavenly realm as the Prophets in the Old Testament did too and we read of the great miracles that resulted through their lives.

I do wonder what is wrong with us today, when we consider all that Jesus has made available to us. Why are we living so far below His provision for us? As for me, I want to see a change in my prayer-life that will result in similar miracles to those we read about from such men of God as Elijah, Elisha, David and Moses. They had encounters with God and lived out what they saw, on earth, and these have been recorded in our Bible. Even the pattern of the tabernacle was received by Moses in prayer.

> *'Who serve unto the example and shadow of heavenly things, as Moses was admonished of God when he was about to make the tabernacle: for, See, saith he, that thou make all things according to the pattern shewed to thee in the mount.'*   (Hebrews 8:5)

Spending time in the presence of God so affected the life of Jesus that it enabled Him to do extraordinary miracles, healings, deliverances and even raise people from the dead. In fact Jesus was so filled with heaven, the joy of heaven, the peace of heaven and the healing power of heaven, that the power and authority in His life was infinitely greater than any sickness, any demon and even the natural physical forces on this earth, so much so that the disciples were afraid and wondered what kind of Man this was that even the wind and the waves obeyed Him.

If only we would seek the Father as Jesus did, He would fill us with *His* power and authority and thus enable us to effectively do His work on earth.

It is up to us.

Some questions to think about:

- 'Believing that God will do it', how does that affect answers to prayer?
- John 14:15–16 enables us to believe in Jesus as Jesus believed God. How will this affect our practical walk?
- *'I am in my Father and you in me and me in you'* (John 14:20). Through the Holy Spirit we can walk as Jesus walked. What does this mean to you?
- Hebrews 3:1 says we are partakers of the Heavenly calling. How can we receive and live from within this realm?

Village church, Bulgaria: Dinka Ucheva had heart problems and a bad leg. She can now walk without her sticks.

The Power of the Holy Spirit

'But the Comforter, which is the Holy Ghost, whom the Father
will send in my name, he shall teach you all things,
and bring all things to your remembrance,
whatsoever I have said unto you.'
(John 14:26)

Here Jesus is speaking directly to us. Jesus had the Father dwelling in His heart but now the Father has sent us the Holy Spirit to dwell in our hearts and that is not all. We have Jesus' promise in John 14:27,

> *'Peace I leave with you, my peace I give unto you: not as the world giveth, give I unto you. Let not your heart be troubled, neither let it be afraid.'*

We have the peace of Jesus dwelling within us. In John 14:28– 29 Jesus says,

> *'Ye have heard how I said unto you, I go away, and come again unto you. If ye loved me, ye would rejoice, because I said, I go unto the Father: for my Father is greater than I. And now I have told you before it come to pass, that, when it is come to pass, ye might believe.'*

Jesus told us everything He was going to do before He went to the cross and He did it, just as He said He would. Why do we have trouble believing what He says He still has to do? We need to believe more and more in faith in all that He has told us to do.

Jesus carries on to encourage us even more in John 15:4–19,

> '*Abide in me, and I in you. As the branch cannot bear fruit of itself, except it abide in the vine; no more can ye, except ye abide in me. I am the vine, ye are the branches: He that abideth in me, and I in him, the same bringeth forth much fruit: for without me ye can do nothing. If a man abide not in me, he is cast forth as a branch, and is withered; and men gather them, and cast them into the fire, and they are burned. If ye abide in me, and my words abide in you, ye shall ask what ye will, and it shall be done unto you. Herein is my Father glorified, that ye bear much fruit; so shall ye be my disciples. As the Father hath loved me, so have I loved you: continue ye in my love. If ye keep my commandments, ye shall abide in my love; even as I have kept my Father's commandments, and abide in his love. These things have I spoken unto you, that my joy might remain in you, and that your joy might be full. This is my commandment, That ye love one another, as I have loved you. Greater love hath no man than this, that a man lay down his life for his friends. Ye are my friends, if ye do whatsoever I command you. Henceforth I call you not servants; for the servant knoweth not what his lord doeth: but I have called you friends; for all things that I have heard of my Father I have made known unto you. Ye have not chosen me, but I have chosen you, and ordained you, that ye should go and bring forth fruit, and that your fruit should remain: that whatsoever ye shall ask of the Father in my name, he may give it you. These things I command you, that ye love one another. If the world hate you, ye know that it hated me before it hated you. If ye were of the world, the world would love his own: but because ye are not of the world, but I have chosen you out of the world, therefore the world hateth you.*'

In John 15:26 Jesus says,

> 'But when the Comforter is come, whom I will send unto you from
> the Father, even the Spirit of truth, which proceedeth from the
> Father, he shall testify of me . . .'

The Holy Spirit has come and has been coming to every
believer who will receive Him for over two thousand years.
Everything that Jesus said in the book of John has come true,
just as true as every miracle He did, every healing He did and
every teaching He has given to us. He is the Truth and He has
proved Himself to us.

The Holy Spirit within us teaches us all we need to know
and brings to our remembrance all we need at any given point
in time. The Holy Spirit also enables us to do the works of
Jesus as we witness to others.

John 16:2–4 gives us a warning that we may need one day,

> 'They shall put you out of the synagogues: yea, the time cometh, that
> whosoever killeth you will think that he doeth God service. And these
> things will they do unto you, because they have not known the
> Father, nor me. But these things have I told you, that when the time
> shall come, ye may remember that I told you of them . . .'

Are we ready to follow Jesus whatever the cost? Let us make
that choice and say 'Yes', for even death cannot separate us
from the love of the Lord.

Dwelling on John 16:2–4 a little more, the Lord showed me
how the umbilical cord must be cut before babies can breathe
on their own and thus all the generations are born in this way.
He then showed me how Adam and Eve were spiritually alive
before they sinned and how the God-given spirit within us
would have worked in a similar way, but the Fall of Man
caused us to be born spiritually dead. Then He showed me

how receiving Jesus as Lord and Saviour restored this silver cord through the Holy Spirit.

Here are some passages to illustrate this:

> *'I drew them with cords of a man, with bands of love: and I was to them as they that take off the yoke on their jaws, and I laid meat unto them.'*   (Hosea 11:4)

> *They shall ask the way to Zion with their faces thitherward, saying, Come, and let us join ourselves to the Lord in a perpetual covenant that shall not be forgotten.'*   (Jeremiah 50:5)

> *'But he that is joined unto the Lord is one spirit.'*
> (1 Corinthians 6:17)

> *'Or ever the silver cord be loosed, or the golden bowl be broken, or the pitcher be broken at the fountain, or the wheel broken at the cistern. Then shall the dust return to the earth as it was: and the spirit shall return unto God who gave it.'*   (Ecclesiastes 12:6–7)

The beautiful things of the earth are fragile and perish but when we have a reverent and loving relationship with our Creator, the spirit within us returns to God who gave it.

> *'Who shall separate us from the love of Christ? Shall tribulation, or distress, or persecution, or famine, or nakedness, or peril, or sword? As it is written, For thy sake we are killed all the day long; we are accounted as sheep for the slaughter. Nay, in all these things we are more than conquerors through him that loved us. For I am persuaded, that neither death, nor life, nor angels, nor principalities, nor powers, nor things present, nor things to come, Nor height, nor depth, nor any other creature, shall be able to separate us from the love of God, which is in Christ Jesus our Lord.'*   (Romans 8:35–39)

These wonderful words show us that when we receive Jesus and His Holy Spirit abides within us, nothing whatsoever can sever our connection with Christ. Our connection with Christ is like a cord that is invisible, yet stronger than steel. For just as death could not separate Jesus from God, so we too cannot be separated from Christ by death, but will return to God in our spirits to live forever with Him.

Living for God therefore becomes our greatest desire on earth and getting to know God more and more brings this to a new dimension.

It is not just living for God but rather living and acting from within the presence of God in joyful obedience formed from our relationship with Him. We learn more and more to see, with Him, what is to be our course of action, knowing He is with us and that He will do what we cannot do, in miracle works and in healing the sick.

This type of service is more a 'teamwork' with God and when it is fully effective it results in much fruit.

Working from within His presence is much more effective than just working for Him. It is only in prayer that we can discover this and then live it out in action.

On one occasion I was called to our ranch to help cast out a demon, which other people had already spent two and a half hours trying to do, but the demon kept challenging them. As I entered the room, the demon pointed directly at me through the man's hand and growled, 'I know who you are. You go around the world preaching the Gospel; I will tear you to pieces'. Suddenly he launched at me like a tiger and I leapt backwards and somersaulted out of his way, as four men pounced on him to get him back onto the ground where they sat on him and held him down. 'I am not going back to the abyss, I am staying right here, for we are legion,' the demons went on, as we carried on trying to cast them out. After thirty minutes of this, I had to leave to teach a riding lesson, so I suggested to the intercessory team that they fast for seven days, get the man to forgive *first*, and only then to cast out the demons, so we bound them down and we ended it there for that day.

Later I approached the Lord to ask why the demons had tried to attack me. It took a full week of seeking the Lord in my quiet time with Him and on the seventh day the Lord showed me Ephesians 4:15,

> 'But speaking the truth in love, may grow up into him in all things, which is the head, even Christ . . .'

and Ephesians 6:10,

> 'Finally, my brethren, be strong in the Lord, and in the power of his might.'

And then He showed me Colossians 2:9–10,

> 'For in him dwelleth all the fulness of the Godhead bodily. And ye are complete in him, which is the head of all principality and power.'

It is only by living **in** Christ through prayer and action that we can attain His authority and power over every demon and every sickness. Without Him we are powerless to do anything and if we are only spending a limited time in God's presence, how can we live fully in Him or have full authority over the demons or sicknesses that we try to cast out in His Name?

It is only when we grow **into** Christ's presence through prayer and lifestyle that we will begin to live **in** His presence, in the heavenly realm, even as we walk this earth. Only as we live **in** Christ, that is, yielded to Him in every area of our lives, knowing His glorious presence by knowing Him through prayer, that we can begin to live our lives from within His presence in effective, victorious work on this earth and gain **in** Christ full victory to cast out every demon and every sickness in the Name of Jesus. This is my goal, to pursue and grow up in Christ in every way, until this is attained in my life and lived out in my life in every way. He is dramatically changing me already.

Every saying of Jesus on 'only doing the Father's will' teaches us different areas that will affect our lives so that we are raised up into a new level of walking in Him. The more we come to know God, the more we will know how to walk in Him as we serve Him in the ministries which He has entrusted to us. To come to know God more also means we must wait on Him more in prayer. Waiting on God is not passive, but is a passion to do His will. It is about waiting on Him for wisdom or instructions as to *how* to do His will, or for an answer to a problem and then for his wisdom for how to deal with it.

As I said in chapter 1, when the Lord told me to reach every village for Him in those countries where He was sending me, I exclaimed, 'That is impossible, even in two lifetimes!' But then the Lord said, 'I will show you how.' So I had to really wait on God to find out 'how' and the Lord revealed that it would be by raising up other evangelists from those countries' own indigenous people and equipping them with Bibles and Bible training, bicycles and megaphones. Evangelists would be sent out on their bicycles to the remote villages to plant churches.

This did not all come all at once but gradually, step by step, over two years and the vision from God grew into over 100 Bible schools with over 4,000 students, spread over eighteen countries. These students have planted thousands of churches in 2008 and are baptising new believers every week. We now have 10,000 students who have registered to study in 2009.

It is our love for God that motivates us to be disciplined about waiting on Him, to find out how to express our love for Him creatively and effectively in service. Without this discipline and focus, we could fail to hear God in some instances and make mistakes. Waiting on God with such intense focus will draw Him to answer us and equip us for the work ahead.

Psalm 37:9 promises,

> 'For evildoers shall be cut off: but those that wait upon the LORD, they shall inherit the earth.'

The Lord is interested in drawing to Himself not just a few groups of people here and there but whole nations. He will link us up with like-minded people to do this and He will speak to others, just as He speaks to us and will join us together to serve Him.

In India the Lord linked me to people who had exactly the same vision which He had given to me and together, and with His help, we are sending evangelists on bicycles to reach every village within the next few years.

The Lord did not leave it there but He encouraged me also. As I was looking at the millions of ripples on a large lake in New Zealand, He gave me a strong impression that each ripple represented an evangelist on a bicycle in India. The next step was to wait on Him with an earnest request as to how all the money for this would be raised. Waiting on the Lord is continuous and out of this His work will be done on earth through you and through me.

Some questions to think about:

- What does John 14:16 mean to you?
- Why is the Holy Spirit given to us?
- Working from within God's presence is more effective than working for Him. Explain.
- How do we live **in** Christ?

The Guidance of the Holy Spirit

'Howbeit when he, the Spirit of truth, is come, he will guide you into all truth: for he shall not speak of himself; but whatsoever he shall hear, that shall he speak: and he will shew you things to come. He shall glorify me: for he shall receive of mine, and shall shew it unto you. All things that the Father hath are mine: therefore said I, that he shall take of mine, and shall shew it unto you.'
(John 16:13–15)

And in that day ye shall ask me nothing. Verily, verily, I say unto you, Whatsoever ye shall ask the Father in my name, he will give it you. Hitherto have ye asked nothing in my name: ask, and ye shall receive, that your joy may be full.
These things have I spoken unto you in proverbs: but the time cometh, when I shall no more speak unto you in proverbs, but I shall shew you plainly of the Father.
At that day ye shall ask in my name: and I say not unto you, that I will pray the Father for you: For the Father himself loveth you, because ye have loved me, and have believed that I came out from God. I came forth from the Father, and am come into the world: again, I leave the world, and go to the Father.'
(John 16:23–28)

Jesus is pointing us to the Father and telling us to ask the Father in His Name and He will give it to us. What more do we ever need? The Holy Spirit, whom the Father has sent to dwell in our hearts, will guide us into all truth and it is wonderful that even the Holy Spirit does nothing of His own accord but only what He sees and hears the Father doing. He will even show us things to come, bring glory to the Father and enable us to do the work that God has called us to do on earth.

When we listen to the Holy Spirit and only do what He shows us, the work He gives us to do for Him is a guaranteed success and it is impossible to fail if we only do what He tells us to do. It is in prayer that we will hear Him and in the practical walk that we obey Him.

The Lord can use any of us who wish to be used by Him. I have given children riding lessons for forty years. For most of that time I lived in jodhpurs and boots, mucked out stables, cared for horses in the rain and mud, and thought this was what I would be doing for the rest of my life. That is until the Lord gave me a different job to do but we still have the riding school for our living. What the Lord is doing now is beyond my wildest dreams: we are running a mobile Bible School of Evangelism with over 4,000 students, who are trained to go out as evangelists and we are raising money for 3,000 bicycles so that they can reach 10,000 remote rural villages and plant churches there this year. Yet the Lord has already done it, because this is God's work, and it is His will that every village in Africa and India be reached with the Gospel before His great return.

If the Lord can use me, He can use you. Will you respond to Him?

In John 17:6–11, we read Jesus' great prayer for His disciples,

> *'I have manifested thy name unto the men which thou gavest me out of the world: thine they were, and thou gavest them me; and they*

have kept thy word. Now they have known that all things whatsoever thou hast given me are of thee. For I have given unto them the words which thou gavest me; and they have received them, and have known surely that I came out from thee, and they have believed that thou didst send me. I pray for them: I pray not for the world, but for them which thou hast given me; for they are thine. And all mine are thine, and thine are mine; and I am glorified in them. And now I am no more in the world, but these are in the world, and I come to thee. Holy Father, keep through thine own name those whom thou hast given me, that they may be one, as we are.'

We know how the disciples went out into the known world at that time and spread His Name far and wide, bringing thousands upon thousands to repentance and to faith in Jesus. We also know of the healings and miracles that accompanied the disciples wherever they went.

Now let us read of Jesus' great prayer for us in John 17:20–26,

'Neither pray I for these alone, but for them also which shall believe on me through their word; That they all may be one; as thou, Father, art in me, and I in thee, that they also may be one in us: that the world may believe that thou hast sent me. And the glory which thou gavest me I have given them; that they may be one, even as we are one: I in them, and thou in me, that they may be made perfect in one; and that the world may know that thou hast sent me, and hast loved them, as thou hast loved me. Father, I will that they also, whom thou hast given me, be with me where I am; that they may behold my glory, which thou hast given me: for thou lovedst me before the foundation of the world. O righteous Father, the world hath not known thee: but I have known thee, and these have known that thou hast sent me. And I have declared unto them thy name, and will declare it: that the love wherewith thou hast loved me may be in them, and I in them.'

What more can I say? There is nothing to add; Jesus has done it all. He has given us everything we will ever need to do His work. Our living Jesus will tell us everything we need to know and give us every word that we are to speak. He will heal every person on whom He has told us to lay hands and do every miracle that is needed to get His work done.

All we have to do is submit to Him and pray earnestly at all times, sharing every detail of our work with Him and asking Him for every need.

Coming into the Lord's presence in prayer is connecting with Him with your heart without words, just a simple, beautiful love connection where He reads your thoughts and you feel His love. You feel His tears for those people He yearns to reach and you simply receive His anointing and gradually even more anointing to do His work. We need to do it His way, with His words, with His method of reaching people, and every day it is different so every day you need to come to God again.

Every day the Lord will renew the fire within your heart. As you spend time communicating with Him, asking Him to meet the needs of people, so He fans the flame within you, until it burns so strongly that nothing will hold you back. Sometimes when you open your mouth, His words come out with such force and such compassion that you are startled. Yes, it is all of Him and none of you. You are simply the vessel through whom He pours His marvellous work.

Sometimes when you really connect with God and He connects with you, He fires you up like an electric bulb and this enables you to connect with the people you speak to in such a way that they respond with one voice to God, and His Holy Spirit breaks forth over the entire group of people and all come into His glorious presence with you. It is then that miracles of healing happen among the people with no laying on of hands and the rejoicing in Him becomes ecstatic.

Let's see what happened to the seventy people Jesus sent out in Luke 10:17–24,

> *'And the seventy returned again with joy, saying, Lord, even the devils are subject unto us through thy name. And he said unto them, I beheld Satan as lightning fall from heaven. Behold, I give unto you power to tread on serpents and scorpions, and over all the power of the enemy: and nothing shall by any means hurt you. Notwithstanding in this rejoice not, that the spirits are subject unto you; but rather rejoice, because your names are written in heaven. In that hour Jesus rejoiced in spirit, and said, I thank thee, O Father, Lord of heaven and earth, that thou hast hid these things from the wise and prudent, and hast revealed them unto babes: even so, Father; for so it seemed good in thy sight. All things are delivered to me of my Father: and no man knoweth who the Son is, but the Father; and who the Father is, but the Son, and he to whom the Son will reveal him. And he turned him unto his disciples, and said privately, Blessed are the eyes which see the things that ye see: For I tell you, that many prophets and kings have desired to see those things which ye see, and have not seen them; and to hear those things which ye hear, and have not heard them.'*

There is a glorious breakthrough one can experience when one truly tries to live doing only the Father's will. In the physical we are so so limited, but, when one rises up in Christ in prayer, dedicated to only do His will, you will become no longer limited.

What you will see in the spiritual realm with the Father will open up different ways of doing things to then achieve far more than one can ever think or imagine.

In the ministry the Lord gave to me is the following chart:

In 2005 with no training, we raised the money to buy 22 bicycles and 54 churches were planted.

In 2006 with 200 evangelists trained, 100 bicycles were bought and they planted 256 churches.

In 2007 with 400 evangelists trained, 301 bicycles were bought and they planted 458 churches.

In 2008 with 4,000 evangelists trained, 1,000 bicycles were bought and they planted 10,000 churches.

In 2009 about 11,000 people have already signed up for training.

Impossible? Not with God, for He Himself has shown me every step. He has provided every need and the power and authority to do it. He has shown me how to network and organise, how to pioneer and establish and bring revival.

On my own, as a girl, definitely impossible, but, when we connect up with the God of the universe, anything is possible and this is reality.

I would like to share with you just one more highlight. My November 2008 trip to India that demonstrates so much that has been written in this book.

News headlines – Cyclone 'Khai mut' is sweeping over Andhra Pradesh and will take at least three days to pass. Already much damage had been done and we are boarding the aircraft.

Upon arriving the cyclone had not yet reached our area, we had supper and then went to bed. At 1.30am I was awoken to the heaviest rain, thunder and lightning I had ever experienced and began to call out to God in earnest, seeing that this could ruin the whole conference and crusade that was all to be held outside. 'Lord, it has cost us so much money to put this crusade together. Only You can stop this cyclone.'

Then I remembered how Jesus rebuked His disciples when He rebuked the storm and then said, 'Peace be still,' and the wind ceased, there was a great calm, and then He said unto them, 'Why are you so fearful? How is it that you have no faith?' Did Jesus expect His disciples to rather rise up and take authority with Him over the storm?

So I began to pray in a different way. I spoke to the cyclone and commanded it to die down in Jesus' name. I rebuked the forces behind the cyclone and bound them down in Jesus name. At 4.00 am the Lord said to me, 'The cyclone will be gone by 6.00 am.' 'Thank You, Lord Jesus,' and I went to sleep. I awoke to a beautiful sunny calm day at 8.00 am. On asking others when the cyclone ended they said 6.00 am. They also said that all the pastors of the crusade had been praying through the night for the cyclone to stop.

This was the start to the most amazing conference and crusade we have ever witnessed. On Monday morning at the pastors' conference, I spoke on the gifts of the Holy Spirit. On Monday afternoon Donna, Peter and I went to the orphanage where the plaque curtain was opened, thereby officially opening the orphanage. On Tuesday I spoke about 'only doing the Father's will', leading onto glorious prayer and worship in response, and on Wednesday the awarding of 1,000 certificates to our graduates and commissioning them as evangelists.

The crusade began on Wednesday night to 20,000 keen people. I spoke on 'Who is Jesus?' 12,640 people stood up to receive Jesus as Lord. I then prayed for the sick; thousands of people then received healing and queued up to testify.

This was shown on Thursday morning on national TV for one hour, and then we opened a new church plant in a village that felt like it was straight out of the Book of Acts. That evening we went to the crusade. 86,000 people crowded the field, and danced and sang with those singing on the platform. I got up and shared 'the three greatest gifts' resulting in 21,640 people receiving Jesus as Lord. We then prayed for the sick and again thousands of people pushed forward to testify of their healings. This was shown the following morning again for another hour on national TV, all free of charge.

On Friday morning, we opened another church plant and dedicated it. In the evening we got stuck in the traffic jam to the crusade, hundreds of tractors and lorries full of people from the villages, buses, overloaded motor bikes, and every form of transport, full of excited people.

Once we reached the grounds, the guards made way for us and ran ahead blowing whistles for us to follow. We quickly get out of the car and walk between guards holding sticks between each other to make a passageway to the platform. 160,000 people were crowded in and more just kept coming as the singers led the worship and danced with exhilarating joy.

I was then called forward to an excited people with the greatest news of the universe: what Jesus had done for them, no frills, no trims, the straight gospel, simple and to the point. 'Who wants to receive this Jesus?' I call out. The entire people rise to their feet. I lead them through the sinner's prayer. The people are serious now and pray out loud ending the prayer with raised hands and thanksgiving.

I tell them to sit down. 'Jesus is right here in the spirit realm and He wants to heal your bodies right where you are, so if you are sick stand up.' Many thousands of people stand. 'Put your own hand on your sickness or your pain and receive your healing now in Jesus' name. Simply say this prayer, "Jesus, put Your hand on my hand and I will be healed." ' They all do so. 'When you are healed put your hand up high in the air.' Thousands of hands go up. 'This is the power of our living Jesus healing you.' I proclaim. Now the people really get excited. They all want to testify and push forward to share, but only a few will be able to, due to lack of time. One lady healed of TB the day before brought her doctor's report: 'No sign of TB left in her body.' So the testimonies of healing followed, while the pastors made prayer tunnels for the people to go through for some prayer due to there being so many people. They then collected their decision cards to post back with their details for follow up. All 60,000 decision cards were collected.

The next day we gave out 582 bicycles to the evangelists who had graduated from our 'Bible School of Evangelism' and had planted seven churches in 2008 to qualify for a bicycle. This ended with a victory ride through town where I joined in for the ride of my life through busy streets, cows, cars, pony carts, people and garlands thrown round my neck. Even the Hindu priests gave their blessings to this half mile long procession of bicycles.

The next morning the bicycle distribution and ride through town was also broadcast for one hour on national TV. I did not even realise we were being filmed. On Saturday and Sunday we spoke in more churches.

On Monday the Post Office phoned Rev. Ganter, 'Please come and clear your mail because it has filled half our post room.' Sure enough 58,632 decision cards were collected and opened plus healings, 14 totally blind people healed – 6 men and 8 women, 29 kidney patients healed – 11 men and 18 women, 16 cancer patients healed – 13 men and 3 women, 2 crippled handicapped people healed – 2 men, and 2 withered hands healed – both were men, and more coming in. I am invited to do another crusade this size in March 2009 and November 2009 in different towns. Over 91,000 conversions already.

As we left we visited the orphans to say goodbye to them, when Ester and her mum arrived late for school. On seeing us there her mum asked us to pray for eleven-year-old Ester who was born deaf and dumb. Peter, Donna and I laid hands on her and within two minutes the Lord healed her she could say her first words. With that we left to catch the plane home.

Three days later I was in Bulgaria and here the Lord gave me a new boldness as we went from village to village to spread the good news of the gospel. The people got so excited as Jesus dissolved cataracts from eyes, opened ears and healed arms and legs so that they could move more freely.

Jesus had God dwelling in Him, but He has given us the

Holy Spirit to dwell in us. He who is in Jesus is stronger than the storms, sicknesses, demons and even death.

We are no longer to be chicken Christians running for cover at the slightest storm, clucking to each other about our rights being taken from us, how godless systems are taking over, cluck, cluck, cluck; but instead we need to face the storm, to become in Christ as eagle Christians, to rise up in Him, and in His authority to take command in Jesus' name in prayer and in action.

We need to do this now before it's really too late. Our God is far greater, far more powerful than we ever know. Our victory is in Him. Not the world but in Him.

In Bulgaria I had a bit of opposition for being a woman evangelist. Well, a woman at least knows how to submit. She knows she is weaker and knows how to depend on God to then only do **His will** and the power that comes through. 'Only doing the Father's will' is enough to change the world, thus the subject of this book.

Basically the nine gifts of the Holy Spirit, which are all supernatural gifts, equip us fully to walk in the supernatural realm or heavenly realm as I have called it in this book.

The unbeliever is born the flesh only. Because he is spiritually dead, cut off from God spiritually due to the fall of man through Adam and Eve, he is limited to live on the natural realm only. The supernatural will therefore make no sense to that person as the supernatural realm is impossible for that person.

But when a person receives Jesus as Lord and Saviour he becomes born to eternal life, a son or daughter of the living God. He therefore does not need to be limited to the natural realm any more, for as the gift of salvation delivers one from sin and by practising the gift of righteousness daily frees one from sin, the gift of the Holy Spirit complete with all nine gifts will equip each one of us to fully live and work from the supernatural realm. Unfortunately many who get baptised in the Holy Spirit receive the gift of tongues and are satisfied with this one gift alone.

The gift of wisdom, the gift of knowledge and the gift of discernment of spirits are yet more wonderful gifts that can be received along with tongues, interpretation of tongues and prophecy.

If we have these six gifts then the gift of healing or the working of miracles become reality through this. The gift of faith to walk in all nine gifts becomes ours as well.

We need to receive all that God wishes to give us if we are to walk in the supernatural realm in God effectively. If you would like to receive a free course on the gifts of the Holy Spirit, please contact me through the e-mail, the phone number and address at the back of this book.

To You

I bow in awe before the Lord, having been allowed to write this book. It appears that the Lord is opening these revelations from Scripture to various prophets across the earth and I believe He is revealing these things for these last days.

The insights that the Lord has given me in this book have become the core of my life as I learn to live 'only doing the Father's will' day-by-day. They have transformed my life, causing the ministry that the Lord has given to me to far exceed every dream, resulting in a very effective work for God.

This book is only a start. There is much more to learn from God and as you spend time in His presence, He will teach you step by step as He is teaching me.

As we listen to His voice and walk in total, joyful, trusting obedience and do that which He has told us to do, we can know with certainty that He will do what we cannot do. He will heal the sick, deliver the people and bring many to Himself and He Himself will supply every need.

Let us learn to pray and come to know our Father more,

just as Jesus has commanded us to do. The more we know Him, the greater our faith will become.

God bless you and keep you. May His love be with you forever.

Some questions to think about:

- The Holy Spirit does not speak of himself but whatsoever he shall hear from the Father. How does this reassure you?
- If the Lord can use me, He can use you. How will you respond?
- Jesus has given us everything we will ever need to do his work as we submit to Him, pray earnestly and ask him for every need. How will this affect you as you respond?
- When we connect with God in prayer, listen to His voice, and walk in total, joyful, trusting obedience, to do what He has told us to do. What will be the result?

Vilka Kolova – knee problems healed – sticks thrown on the ground.

For a full list of books plus free teaching on the gift of the
Holy Spirit contact Suzanne Pillans at:

Suzanne's Ministries
Standlake Equestrian Centre and Ranch
Downs Road, Standlake, Oxfordshire OX29 7UH

Website: **www.suzannesministries.co.uk**
Email: **wpillans@aol.com**

Other books by Suzanne Pillans

Dare to Follow – How to follow God in obedience.

Dare to Step Out in Faith – How to rise up to our potential.

Dare to Enter His Presence – Step by step into His presence.

Heaven Sent Riding Skills – Riding a horse God's way.

DVD sets by Suzanne Pillans

Dare to Do Only the Father's Will
12 lessons with healings – £15.

The Foundations of Our Faith
14 lessons with practical – £15.

The Holy Spirit and Prayer –
12 lessons with results.

Gift DVDs

The India Crusade (2008) to 160,000 people plus healings – £6.

The Leaders' Summit (2008) – preparing a leader – £6.

Health & Home – healing and Suzanne's story –
ideal for unbelievers – £4.

Introduction to Suzanne's Ministry – **free** with your order.